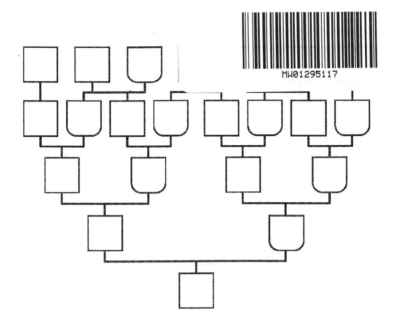

ENDOGAMY: ONE FAMILY, ONE PEOPLE

Israel Pickholtz

Helping You Grow Your Family Tree

ISBN 978-1-68034-038-9

Colonial Roots
Millsboro, Delaware
First printing, July 2015

This volume is dedicated to

My first cousin once removed Merissa Mahoy,
whose inquiry is behind all the serious genealogy I have ever done.
She was nine years old at the time.

The first family members who agreed to do DNA tests:
My aunt Betty Goldman, my father's cousin Herb Braun
and my friend and probable fourth cousin Dalia Pickholz Kaplan
and her husband Menachem.
They gave me the confidence to do what followed.

The memory of the late, great Betty Lee (Buzy) Hahn,
my Denver third cousin, who introduced me to Skalat.

The memory of my great-grandfather's uncle, Selig Pikholz,
and my father, who remembered hearing his name.

Table of Contents

FOREWORD

In the last few years, many volumes have been produced about genetic genealogy. That is no wonder because the field is both growing in popularity and developing rapidly with new tools and new methods. But I have not seen anything on the genetic genealogy of Jews and other "closed" populations.

The purpose of this book is to change that.

European Jews have always married mainly within the tribe. Whether our numbers five hundred years ago in Europe were four hundred or four hundred thousand, the pool was limited. As a result, the members of the tribe today are all related to one another multiple times. This phenomenon, known as endogamy, makes Jewish genetic genealogy very difficult, often impossible. There is a similar phenomenon in other population groups.

I was convinced that this brick wall is not as impenetrable as it seems, at least in some circumstances.

I believe that this book demonstrates that I was correct.

When I decided I wanted to write a book, I was not sure if I wanted to write a "How to" book or a "How I did it" book. The decision was dictated by the facts in the field. Different family structures, widely different numbers of living family members, and other similar factors dictated that writing "How to" would be irrelevant for most researchers.

"How I did it" is more likely to be helpful to the research community and more likely to instill the confidence necessary for such a project.

It is my hope that this book will encourage and inspire other researchers of their European Jewish families and other endogamous populations to say "I can do this!"

Israel Pickholtz
Jerusalem
5775/2015

ACKNOWLEDGEMENTS

There are so many people I want to acknowledge and thank. This is a work about genetic genealogy, so I have decided to limit the acknowledgements to three categories:

- Those whose encouragement has brought me to this point
- Those whose assistance in matters of DNA has helped me get to where I think I have something to say
- A few others

Many who have participated in and supported my genealogy work over the years are mentioned in the text. Their appearance there is a reflection of my appreciation.

Any errors of style, syntax, fact, or judgment are my own. I made my own decisions despite sometimes having been advised otherwise.

Encouragement

My first genealogy mentor, Carol Skydell, formerly Vice-President of JewishGen.

I spoke of my plans for a DNA testing project to Pamela Weisberger while she was visiting Israel in 2012. She encouraged me to submit a presentation for Boston.[1] I did and it was well-received, though even when I presented my talk, I had very few results to report. From there it has been a runaway train.

Dvora Netzer and Dalia and Menachem Kaplan previewed an early (Hebrew) version of my Boston presentation. They thought it worked.

Emily Aulicino, the author of *Genetic Genealogy—The Basics and Beyond*, who challenged me to write a book and who held my hand through the early decision process.

Melody Amsel Arieli, a real, published writer who helped show me the ropes.

My wonderful Facebook friends who give me encouragement with every post and every blog and make me feel that I actually know what I am doing. You know who you are!

The people of DNA analysis

Elissa Scalise Powell, CG, CGL, Co-Director of the Genealogical Research Institute of Pittsburgh who organized the course in Practical Genetic Genealogy, July 2014.

The wonderful teachers of that course, Blaine Bettinger, CeCe Moore and Debbie Parker Wayne, for their teaching and for their emphasis on the notion that "citizen scientists" must not be afraid to challenge the prevailing consensus. Also for putting up with me as a student, and for being available in the months following.

Kitty Cooper who sat with me for more than two hours in Salt Lake City, whose analytical tools have helped me organize myself and who has given me her thoughts whenever I have asked.

Roberta Estes, whose blog *dna-explained.com* analyzes DNA and brings examples from her own ancestry. Roberta, I have learned much from you, and your encouragement has been most valuable.

Curtis Rogers, John Olsen and Jim Bartlett of GEDmatch for providing tools and responding patiently to my questions and comments.

The Family Tree DNA family with special thanks to the incredibly competent and patient Janine Cloud, who surely deserves a raise.

Dr. Richard Pavelle, who made his MtDNA data available for comparison.

A few others

Amy and Ron Kritzman, who have provided the server and the domain name which is *pikholz.org*.

Sarajoy Pickholtz, who turned my title and design idea into the cover of this book, and who designed the book's website and took over the responsibility for all the graphics, and made my crude charts work.

My cousin Howard Goldman for the cartoon in Chapter Ten.

Gold Medal Ideas.

Alex Sharon who knows every name of every town and village in east Galicia. John Steed of Brother's Keeper, who has been patiently answering my questions for nearly twenty years.

My friends Lara Diamond and Zvi Ofer, whose comments were always forthright and on point.

My publisher, the incredibly patient Debbie Hooper of Colonial Roots, who has done everything I could ask and more. And to her editor, Josie, who saved me from showing the world that I do not understand hyphenation and consistency of tense. We genealogists use present tense verbs, even when referring to people who have been dead for a hundred fifty years.

My writer-friend, neighbor, and fellow Yinzer, Varda Meyers Epstein, reviewed this manuscript before submission as she so graciously reviews most of my published writing. Varda is also the person who pushed me into the world of writing.

My wife Frances, of the London Silbersteins, who has been generally patient and allowed me to block out the time necessary for this writing and who has encouraged me to use funds for DNA testing—funds which might have been used for other purposes.

---

[1] The 33rd International Association of Jewish Genealogical Societies (IAJGS) International Conference on Jewish Genealogy was held in Boston, 4-9 August 2013.

INTRODUCTION
How Did I Get Here?

Listening

Before there was a viable option for genetic genealogy, there was just the Internet with its online databases, search engines, and discussion groups.

Before there was Internet, there was gumshoe research in archives, libraries, and cemeteries, with personal interviews and stamp-and-envelope inquiries and correspondence.

But before there was any research at all, there were stories. And if we were lucky, our elders talked even before we knew how to ask questions. Some of us listened and paid attention.

When I was about eight, we drove from Pittsburgh to Washington D.C. to visit Mother's cousins. Mother told us who was who, and I drew boxes in my head with connecting lines.

One day when I was eleven or twelve, Nana, my father's mother, said to me *ex-nihilo* "My mother-in-law had ten children, not just the seven you know." I wondered about the other three, but never asked.

When I began what I then thought was real genealogy, my father told me that his paternal grandfather—who died when my father was eight—had an uncle named Selig Pikholz. It is not remarkable that my father told me this. What is remarkable is that he knew it at all. I have never found anyone else in the family who knew this bit of information. My father also listened and paid attention.

Then in 1993 at Nana's ninetieth-birthday party, my cousin Karen's nine-year old daughter Merissa—whom I had never met before and have not seen since—asked me if I would give her a copy of what I had learned about the family tree. I was not about to admit that I had done nothing for more than a dozen years except collect a drawer full of notes, so I borrowed a copy of Brother's Keeper 4.5[1] and have been running ever since.

Starting point

All four of my grandparents were in the United States before World War I. My father's father's family came to Pittsburgh in four stages in the period from 1901 to 1904. My grandfather, the youngest, was seven.

Nana's family was better off financially. Her father, Moritz Rosenzweig, went to Pittsburgh in 1901 and his wife and children followed him together sixteen months later. Nana, the youngest, was born in what is now Pittsburgh.[2]

Mother's father, Rachmiel Gordon, went to New York in 1906 after his mother died. His brother and two sisters lived in Brooklyn and Washington.

Mother's mother, Sarah Rosenbloom, went to New York in 1910. She too had two sisters in New York but by 1916, both were dead. Her younger brother was at sea when World War I began, and eventually he lived in Washington D.C. My grandmother left her father (my namesake), a sister, a half-sister, and a half-brother in Russia. She and my grandfather married in New York and moved to Vandergrift in Westmoreland County outside Pittsburgh.

I knew many of these older relatives, although not until I was in my twenties did I actually talk to any of them. By then there were not many left. I was planning to make aliyah (move to Israel) in 1972 and decided I should gather whatever was available. Since I really had no idea what I was doing, I did not ask the right questions. For instance, I asked about names but never about places.

I thought I was being very clever when trying to talk to Mother's father who was not really able, at age eighty-five, to hold a conversation. I asked him what his grandfather's name was, and he didn't respond. But when I said "Your father was Herschel ben (son of) ...," he immediately answered "Mordche."

One great stroke of luck was at my grandfather's funeral in Washington in 1972 where I met his much younger second cousin Sig Fritz. The families were close enough that my grandparents were buried in the plots adjacent to Sig's mother. Sig knew all about our Gordons, and we spent a pleasant evening on the floor of his home going over the huge chart that he had drawn back to his (and my grandfather's) great-grandfather, with me taking notes. Sig's daughter, my third cousin once removed, lives in Jerusalem about a fifteen-minute walk from us, and I call her "my closest living relative."

Before my aliyah I also visited my great-grandparents' graves in two separate cemeteries in Pittsburgh, so I knew their fathers' names from the tombstones. I have since learned their mothers' names, and for three of my father's four grandparents I know some additional generations. But on the Pickholtz line, I still cannot go back further than what I knew forty-odd years ago.

This is as good a time as any to point out that spelling is generally not important. My great-grandfather was "Pickholz" coming off the boat and became "Pickholtz" in Pittsburgh. Almost all the American immigrant families use one of those two spellings. But in mid-to-late 1800s Galicia it was "Pikholz," and that is the spelling I use when referring to the family as a whole and in my website and email. In my writing, I use all three. Other family branches use Pikholc and Pikholtz, and there are documents with any number of misspellings.

Once in Israel, I had some bits and pieces of correspondence with older relatives. But until Merissa came along, this is all I knew of my ancestors.

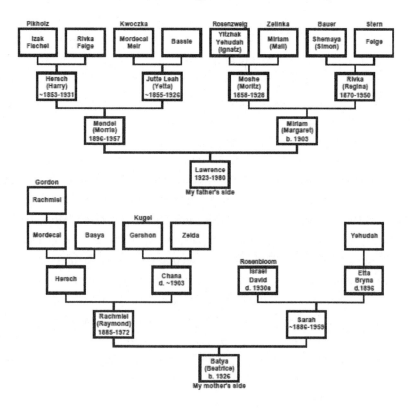

Figure i-1

The Pikholz Project

In early 1996, I met the Internet in general and the discussion group[3] at *JewishGen* in particular. I inquired and searched mostly about my mother's Rosenblooms and Kugels and my father's Rosenzweigs, Zelinkas and Bauers and took some baby steps. And I looked for traces of my Pikholz great-grandfather's sister's family in Denver. I was under the impression that the parts of Eastern Europe where the Pikholz family lived were inscrutable, and that no records were available.

In 1997 and 1998 came the real progress. In August 1997, my cousin Jerry and his wife Marcia had visited from Maryland and told me that at the Children's Memorial at Yad Vashem, they heard the name "Pickholtz" among those piped in to the exhibit. That led me to Yad Vashem's Pages of Testimony.[4] They said they had twenty Pikholz Pages.

A few months later a research colleague, Shuki Ecker, phoned me to say that he was at Yad Vashem and had found eighty-some others. Would I pay for them? I did and began looking for the submitters and other traces of all these people I had never heard of. Many were from places in east Galicia[5] called Skalat and Rozdol—places that were unfamiliar to me.

In August of 1998, Rita Margolies posted on *JewishGen* mentioning her grandmother's brother Shoil Pikholz.

That same month, I received a letter from a woman in the U.S. asking on behalf of one Matthew Brooks about his great-grandfather Harry Pickholtz.

In November, Irene Scharf posted on *JewishGen* mentioning her great-grandmother Bessie Pickholtz.

In December Jacob Laor, here in Israel, posted about his Pikholz family from Klimkowce.

It was clear that the time had come to see what we could do on my father's paternal side.

Soon after, I met with Jacob Laor and Efraim Pickholz (1918-2003), and the Pikholz Project was born. They had already acquired some sixty Pikholz records from the archives in Lwow, and we decided to join forces. I entered all the Pikholz information we had into Brother's Keeper 5.2 as it was clear to me that it was likely that our unusual and uncommon surname probably represented only one or two distinct families.

Efraim knew that his family was from Rozdol, a bit north of Stryj, while Jacob's family was from east of Tarnopol. Irene and Rita's families were from the same area as Jacob's. I hadn't a clue where mine were from. My grandfather's last surviving sister, Aunt Mary, had told me twenty years earlier that she was born in Zelozitz, which I learned later was the Yiddish name for Zalosce, northwest of Tarnopol.

In the meantime, I found the Denver cousins, in particular my third cousin Betty Lee (Buzy) Hahn. She knew that her grandmother had been born in Skalat and a year later invited me to join her on a visit to Galicia. Efraim joined us, and in May 2000, the three of us spent a week doing day trips from Lwow, visiting towns and cemeteries, speaking with mayors and people in the street, all under the supervision of Alex Dunai, guide par excellence.

Jacob and I charged ahead, ordering dozens of records from the AGAD[6] archives in Warsaw that held many of the birth, death, and marriage records for east Galicia.

We determined that the Pikholz families had two centers in the mid-1800s—Rozdol and Skalat, about a three hour drive apart under today's conditions. We took as a given that all the Rozdolers were a single family descended from a known couple who lived in the early 1800s, and that all the Skalaters were descended from an older, unknown couple. We hadn't a clue whether the two families were connected to one another. The pattern of given names didn't overlap. In time, I came to the conclusion that they were probably two different families, but I continued to do research and acquire records for both.

Then the award-winning Jewish Records Indexing-Poland (JRI-Poland) began indexing AGAD, and we began seeing Pikholz descendants in towns across east Galicia. Stanley Diamond of JRI-Poland and Mark Halpern, the director of the AGAD project, were helpful every step of the way.

After several years of work, the structure of the families began to take shape. In some lines, we were able to go back as far as the very late 1700s. In a few, we barely got out of the 1900s. The problem was connecting them to one another. The mission of the Pikholz Project is "to identify and reconnect all Pikholz descendants," but there was a double wall. First, there were few records before 1850 and none back into the 1700s.

Second was the matter of surnames. They barely existed until the 1800s, and even then, surnames were not treated with much respect. A family of five brothers in the late 1700s could have taken five different surnames. And in Galicia, many kosher Jewish marriages were not registered with the civil authorities so the children were given the mother's surname.

I could tell you much more about those pre-DNA days, but my purpose here is to describe where we were in our research when we began with DNA. So here are the Skalat and Rozdol families as we saw them at the beginning of 2011. There are also some individuals and small families that could have come from either place, and I shall work some of them into the story as we go along.

The Kwoczkas

My great-grandfather Hersch Pickholz was married to Jute Leah (Yetta in the U.S.) Kwoczka. As records became available, we found almost everyone with this surname in one place—Zalosce, where my grandfather's family were born. It appears that this Jewish surname is unique to Zalosce[7] and goes back to Jossel and Jute Leah who were born in the mid-1790s and died around 1850. It may be that Kwoczka is a local variation of Kaczka or Kaczor which are common in Skalat—all three of these similar-sounding names being related to poultry.

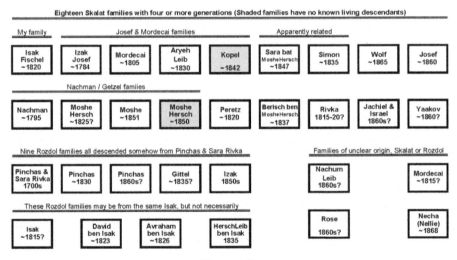

Figure i-2

It appeared from the records that Hersch, his brother, and two sisters were from nearby Podkamen and two of the four married people from Zalosce.

The other two married Skalaters; one couple lived in Zalosce, and the other lived in Skalat before going to the United States.

Jute Leah appears to have had three brothers, Pinchas, Yosef (or probably Avraham Yosef) and Rachmiel. Yosef died at age twenty-five leaving a daughter and a pregnant wife. The daughter died soon after, and we know nothing of the son Yosef born after his father's death.

Two of Pinchas' daughters went to the United States, and thanks to Mrs. Edith Spungen (1924-2010), who is related to (and named for) Pinchas' wife, I developed excellent personal connections with several of that family.

Rachmiel went to the United States and has quite a few descendants who I have been in touch with off and on. Mostly off. One successful connection is with Rachmiel's youngest grandson, Baruch. Baruch's sister found her family listed in my database at the Diaspora Museum in Tel Aviv and contacted me. Baruch and I have become fast friends. He is a second cousin of my father's but is several years younger than I.

There is, however, a small problem with Rachmiel. Jute Leah's grave identifies her father as Mordecai Meir, and that name appears among Pinchas' descendants as well. But Rachmiel's New York tombstone calls his father Mordecai, without a second name. So either Rachmiel's tombstone is incorrect or Mordecai Meir and Mordecai are two different people, calling into question the "one Kwoczka family in Zalosce" theory.

Izak Fischel

My great-great-grandfather was Izak Fischel.[8] That name appears on the tombstone of his daughter Bessie and in various Galician documents. His wife was called both Rivka Feige and Feige Rivka in documents, but my grandfather's sister was named for her as Rivka Feige, so that is what I shall use here.

Although the Jews of Galicia did not always record their marriages with the civil authorities, occasionally a registration will show up many years after the date of the actual Jewish marriage. One such record is the 1887 marriage in Skalat of Berl, age 71, son of Josef and Rojse Pikholz, to Dwojre, age 50, daughter of Motie (=Mordecai) and Taube Pikholz.

This couple had ten children, and there are a few living descendants.

Motie has a grandson named Itzig Josef from one of his other daughters, which led me to surmise that this was a close-cousin marriage or perhaps an uncle-niece. Although I made notes to that effect, I did not record a relationship between Motie and Josef since I had no evidence.

I never found anything else about Rojse, but I found what appear to be death records for the other three. Motie died in 1864 at age fifty-nine, and he would have been born about 1805. Taube died in 1872 at age seventy, so would have been born about 1802. Josef—or more properly, Isak Josef—died in 1862 at age seventy-eight.

If Josef was in fact twenty-one years older than Motie, they could have been father and son, or brothers, or uncle and nephew. Perhaps they were not closely related at all—just two Pikholz from Skalat whose children (also twenty-one years apart) married one another.

Motie had two other daughters and some sons, but I found no other children for Josef. My grandfather had a brother Joseph, who was also born Isak Josef, which made me think that my own family is closely related to this group.

It was then that I found the only Selig Pikholz in my database. Selig had a son Itzik Josef, born in 1862 several months after the death of the old Isak Josef. This indicated to me that Selig was very likely a son or grandson of Isak Josef. I later found that Selig had an older son Markus (= Mordecai, almost certainly), the same given name as Selig's father-in-law. That precluded the possibility that Selig was a son of Motie, who was still alive when Selig's Markus was born. Over time, I found a few more individuals in this family.

My first thought was that Motie was an older brother of my Isak Fischel and Selig, and that all three were sons of Isak Josef. But that was not possible, for Isak Josef would not have had a son named Isak Fischel. No Galician Jew would have invoked the Evil Eye by giving even part of his own name to his son.

But my father had said that Selig Pickholz was his grandfather's uncle, and that left one possibility. Selig must have been the brother of Rivka Feige, not Isak Fischel, and she and Selig would have been the children of Isak Josef. What was Isak Fischel's surname—the surname that should have been mine? I had no idea, but the scenario made sense. Rivka Feige came from Skalat, but her children were born in Podkamen. Perhaps Isak Fischel was from Podkamen or someplace nearby, someplace with no records mentioning his name.

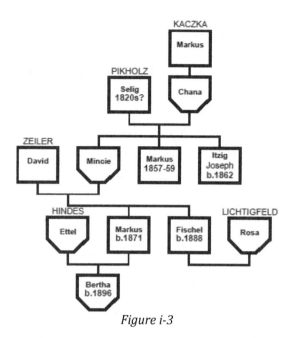

Figure i-3

I did not go so far as to record Selig as a brother of Rivka Feige and a son of Isak Josef, but I was fairly sure he was just that. Hence, the broken line segments in Figure i-4.

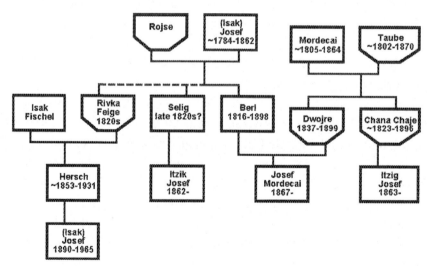

Figure i-4

That left the question of Isak Fischel's surname. It could have been anything, but I knew it wasn't Pikholz. I searched in every way I could think of, including ordering every record from AGAD mentioning the name Isak Fischel or Fischel Yitzhak,[8] to no avail. It has been years, and appears to be a puzzle that would not be solved.

In desperation, I ordered a Y-67 DNA test from Family Tree DNA.[9] This test would show me anyone who matches my male line up to as many as sixty-seven markers. Perhaps someone would show up as a very good match—someone with whom I have a common ancestor within the last two hundred and fifty years or so.

While I was at it, I ordered an MtDNA test of my mother's female line. We know nothing of my mother's maternal grandmother save her given name Etta Bryna, her date of death, and that her father was Yehudah, a Levi.

I placed the order for the two tests in March 2011, and the early results told me nothing useful. But that changed.

In the following chapters, I shall tell you how my family's DNA project came to be, how it came to have more than seventy participants, and how it produced results that I would not have reached had I stuck to the traditional genealogy research tools. Almost every chapter will tell a success story, explaining the background, the process, and the solutions. Since DNA is rarely a complete solution, these chapters will be about more than DNA; they will discuss genetic genealogy as part of genealogy research.

Almost none of the stories I will tell, dear reader, will fit your own research precisely. Your challenges are not identical to mine. Your research goals may not be the same as mine. You do not have precisely the same family members as I. And your DNA cannot be predicted to produce the same kinds of matches as mine.

I am not here to give you a recipe. I am here to give you confidence. I am here to show you that there are ways to approach the challenges of endogamy and that it is possible to achieve success—not for every puzzle, but for many of them. Even solving one of your challenges will make this book worthwhile.

I am not here to discuss the "kohen gene," which is much-discussed in the field. The only Pikholz descendants who are relevant to that either daughtered out or were killed in the Holocaust. One of their female Pikholz ancestors married a kohen, Salamon Lerner, but he and his children went by Pikholz.

Nor am I here to discuss genetic testing for health or medical purposes, though the people who test for that purpose add to the pool of possible matches.

Finally, I am not here to find "deep roots." I do not need DNA to tell me that I am Jewish through and through. We Jews are indeed more than one people, we are one family, as are other closed populations to one degree or another. As far as I am concerned, the claims of the testing companies to identify deep roots by percentages is merely a marketing tool.

I am here to inspire you, to show you what can be done, to encourage you to say "I can do this."

So now you know why I am here. As you continue reading, you will learn how it is that I finally decided what I want to be when I grow up. I look forward to telling you the story.

If you would like to view the images in this book in greater detail, you can download them from my website at www.endogamy-one-family.com/extras.

---

[1] Brother's Keeper upgraded its DOS program to version 5.2 before its first Windows version. I still use the DOS version.

[2] Nana was born in the city of Allegheny, which is now Pittsburgh's North Side.

[3] I use the singular because *JewishGen*'s SIGs (Special Interest Groups) did not have their own lists. There was only the one, which had maybe sixty posts a day.

[4] Yad Vashem, The Holocaust Martyrs and Heroes Remembrance Authority in Jerusalem, collects Pages of Testimony submitted by family and friends of Jews murdered in the Holocaust. The information on these Pages is valuable for research and often provides a living contact who actually knew the particular victims.

[5] The three provinces Lwow, Tarnopol, and Stanislawow make up east Galicia. This is where the Pikholz and Kwoczka families lived in the 1800s. It was part of the Austrian Empire before WWI and afterwards was part of the reconstituted Polish state. It is now the northwest corner of Ukraine.

[6] AGAD, Archiwum Glowne Akt Dawnych (The Central Archives of Historical Records), is located in Warsaw and is the branch of the Polish State Archives that holds most of the Jewish records for east Galicia.

[7] There are Kwoczkas in other parts of Poland, but they are Gentiles.

[8] Occasionally Izak Fischel is called Fischel Yitzhak, but that is not an important difference. On the tombstones of his son (my great-grandfather) and daughter in Pittsburgh, he is called "Izak Yeroham Fischel." Fischel is the Yiddish equivalent of both Efraim and Yeroham, so the Pittsburgh stones merely inform us that he was Yeroham, not Efraim. I shall be referring to him here as "Izak Fischel."

[9] My choice of Family Tree DNA, rather than one of the other testing companies, was based on the services they offered, their prices, and how comfortable I was working with them. I was not planning to write this book at that time, and their management is not aware of my writing it now. Therefore, I obviously have received no consideration from them for the mentions of the company here.

Chapter Zero

DNA Testing 101

Genetic material

Someday, we will be able to discuss genetic genealogy the way we discuss census records and passenger manifests and tombstones—by going straight to the point with explanations included in the text where called for. Genetic genealogy is not yet at that stage, and it is still necessary to review, or for some introduce, the basics. I have called this "Chapter Zero" so the more experienced among you can skip it if you wish.

It is not my intention to discuss the deep science of the chromosomes and genes or the processes that govern their transmission from parents to children. These are relevant to genetic genealogy, but not at the level that I shall be discussing here. This chapter is for the really basic background.

Molecules of deoxyribonucleic acid (DNA) contain genetic instructions for the functioning of all living things in our world. They consist of two coiled strands arranged in a double helix based on the four nucleotides adenine, cytosine, guanine and thymine, known as A, C, G, and T.

DNA is organized into chromosomes and other genetic material within the cells of an organism, mostly in the cell's nucleus.

In humans, genetic material passes from parents to children, so there are similarities between the parents and the children and among the various children of the same parents. By the same token, there are similarities in genetic material among cousins of varying degrees and between a person and his ancestors and their siblings.

For our purposes, there are four categories of genetic material which we can test—Y-chromosomes, mitochondrial DNA (MtDNA), autosomal DNA (atDNA) and X-chromosomes.

I shall be discussing the tests offered by Family Tree DNA (FTDNA) because that is the testing company on which my own work is based. There are two other major testing companies—Ancestry and 23andMe. I have read about their qualities and deficiencies, but I have not yet worked with them myself. I shall say a few words about them at the end of this chapter.

Y-chromosome

The Y-chromosome is what defines males. Men receive them from their fathers. Women do not have them at all, but a woman can learn about her father's Y-chromosome by testing her brother, her father's brother, or certain cousins.

The Y and X-chromosomes are the twenty-third pair of chromosomes, are located in the nucleus of each cell, and they are referred to as the sex chromosomes.

The Y-chromosome usually passes intact, but every few generations a mutation will occur so a man may well have a slightly different Y-chromosome from that of his great-great-grandfather. For that matter, if the mutation has occurred in a man's father's generation, his Y-chromosome may be slightly different from that of his father and brothers.

In the past, FTDNA has offered tests of different levels—12, 25, 37, 67, or 111 markers, but the 12 and 25 are no longer available. Results are in the form of a list of matches, showing for each marker how many mutations have taken place since a common ancestor. For instance, if Moshe and David each take a Y-37 test and the results show a genetic distance of two, it means that two mutations have occurred in their genetic makeup since their most recent common ancestor. Both mutations may have been in Moshe's Y-chromosome or David's, or there may have been one mutation each.

If you are trying to determine whether two men have a recent common ancestor, it is often sufficient to take the minimal test because if they do not match you have your result.

On the other hand, if two men match perfectly at the Y-37 level, all it tells you is that they are 93 percent likely to have a common ancestor within six generations. If they both upgrade to Y-67 and remain identical, the likelihood will rise to nearly 97 percent, but there is no way to be more precise than that. Moshe and David cannot know, based solely on their identical Y-chromosomes, if they are fourth cousins or eighth cousins, or perhaps even first cousins.

In the last few years, FTDNA has been offering several more sophisticated (and expensive) Y-chromosome tests that relate mostly to deep ancestry. That subject and those tests are beyond the scope of this book.

Keep in mind that of your sixteen great-great-grandparents, the Y-chromosome is relevant to only one—your father's father's father's father. So while it is the most straightforward of the tests, the Y-chromosome test is limited in its usefulness. It is, however, a convenient test because the Y-chromosome generally follows the surname, at least to the extent that both pass from father to son without change.

Mitochondrial DNA (MtDNA)

MtDNA is located outside the nucleus of the cell and is arranged in a ring. Both women and men have MtDNA, but since only women pass it to their children, it can be used only on the all-maternal line. Unlike the Y-test, the MtDNA test can be taken by either men or women.

MtDNA mutates far less frequently than Y-DNA, and a perfect match may indicate nothing more than a very distant common female ancestor. That remoteness makes it very hard to find the paths to the common ancestor. This task is harder still because women's surnames generally change when they marry, so you do not have the surname path to guide your research.

MtDNA is limited because, like the Y, it follows the line to only one great-great-grandparent out of sixteen. Therefore, unless you can determine that a perfect match is fairly close, it is usually of very limited value.

FTDNA offers two levels of MtDNA tests—the "plus" version and the "full sequence." Like the Y-DNA test, the more basic, less expensive "plus" test can be useful to eliminate possible matches, but aside from that, it will not take you very far.

That said, I shall discuss some limited, or potential, success that I have had with MtDNA testing, in subsequent chapters.

Autosomal DNA

The twenty-two pairs of chromosomes residing in the nucleus of the cell are called "autosomal DNA." A child gets one set of twenty-two from the mother and the other set from the father. Therefore, every person's DNA consists of fifty percent of the DNA from each parent.

FTDNA cannot tell you what is from which parent, so the fact that you match someone is not enough to tell you if the match is on your mother's or your father's side—or for that matter, if it's on the mother's or father's side of the person you match.

If you are looking at possible matches on your mother's side, her DNA is better than yours because yours is diluted by fifty percent by your father's genetic material. This is different from the Y-DNA and MtDNA tests where it doesn't much matter if you test yourself or your child or parent, providing the gender of the person tested is appropriate to the test.

How the parent passes DNA to the child is not straight-forward and does not follow a simple recipe. Your father has two sets of twenty-two chromosomes, one from your grandfather, and one from your grandmother. What is the single set he passes to you? Some combined version of the two of them that has become a new, (usually) unique chromosome. This new chromosome is on average half from each grandparent, but it can be more from one than from the other. In fact, you can get chromosomes that are mostly or even totally from one of the grandparents.

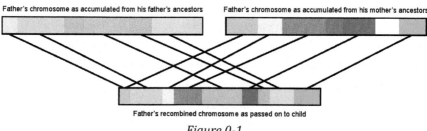

Father's recombined chromosome as passed on to child

Figure 0-1

The creation of the chromosomes that pass to the child is called **recombination** and the process is called **meiosis**. In the simplest terms, each new recombined chromosome that pass on to the child is composed of segments that came from each parent. The locations on the chromosome do not change, so say a segment at the far right end of the child's chromosome #8 must have come from the far right end of chromosome #8 of one of the parents.

Each recombination event is independent, so what a parent passes on to one child will be different from what the same parent passes on to other children. Therefore, on average two siblings share fifty percent of their DNA unless, of course, they are identical twins. Non-identical twins are no different from any other siblings where DNA is concerned.

While a person receives exactly fifty percent of his DNA from each parent, he receives on average twenty-five percent from each grandparent, on average 12.5 percent from each great-grandparent, on average 6.25 percent from each great-great-grandparent, and so on. But because we get to very small percentages after five or six generations, the DNA of some of those ancestors will disappear entirely.

The advantage of autosomal testing (which FTDNA calls "Family Finder") over Y-DNA and MtDNA testing is that it reflects all ancestral lines—all sixteen great-great-grandparents, all thirty-two great-great-great-grandparents—as opposed to one each for the other two tests. But that is also its weakness. Each ancestor is represented by only a small amount of DNA, and no segments are labeled "Great-Grandma Rachel."

Some of a person's segments may come intact from an ancestor eight or ten or twenty generations ago, and since endogamous populations share distant ancestors we must be very careful before accepting a match as proof of recent ancestry. Such a match may be more distant on a different side of the family entirely. This is the problem of endogamy. It is also what demonstrates for all intents and purposes that as one people, we are one family.

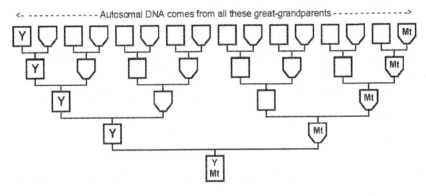

Figure 0-2

When cousins marry

Cousins who marry each other bring genetic material from their mutual ancestors. This results in an overrepresentation of those ancestors' DNA in the cousins' children compared to the other ancestors.

Figure 0-3 shows an example referring to first cousins.

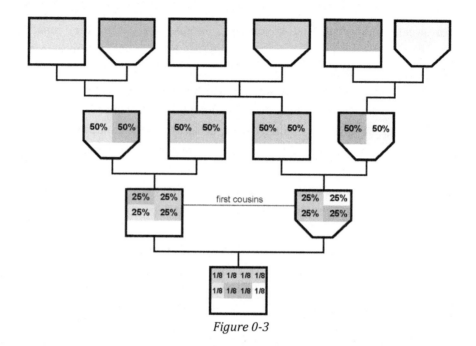

Figure 0-3

The couple in grey and orange in the top row have children in the second row who have half from each parent. Each of those children passes fifty percent of his DNA to the next generation (third row). In this case, they do not pass on exactly half of each parent, which means the 25 percent is an average. Each grandchild in the third row has an average of 25 percent of the grey grandparent and about 25 percent of the orange grandparent.

The great-grandchild has on average half the DNA of each component of his parents—one-eighth from each great-grandparent. But as the figure shows, there are two grey bits and two orange bits—one of each from each parent. The great-grandchild, therefore, has on average one-eighth of his DNA from each of four great-grandparents and one-quarter from the other two.

When this happens often with cousins of various degrees of closeness, and it happens throughout the population, we have endogamy. Good luck figuring out which bits came from which ancestors. That is the problem this book means to address.

X-chromosome

The Y-chromosome is referred to as a sex chromosome because it determines that the person is a male. The male's pair of twenty-third chromosomes contains one Y and one X. For females, both twenty-third chromosomes are X.

The pattern of X-chromosome inheritance is more complicated than any of the others. A male has one X that he receives from his mother. From his father, he receives a Y. The X that he receives from his mother is a recombination of her two X chromosomes—that is the male has one X chromosome derived from the genetic material from his two maternal grandparents.

Women have two X chromosomes. One comes from the mother, which is the standard recombination from her mother's parents. This is no different from what the male received from his mother. The female receives the father's X completely intact since there is nothing for it to recombine with. Her paternal X-chromosome is therefore only from her grandmother, not at all from her grandfather. Another way of looking at it is that no genetic material from an X-chromosome can pass through two consecutive generations of males.

You can see this in Figure 0-4, which represents the inheritance pattern of the X-chromosome. The percentages less than 50 percent are averages.

The female's total of her two X chromosomes—that which recombines to be passed to her children—is composed of (on average) 25 percent each from her two maternal grandparents and her two great-grandparents on her father's mother's side.

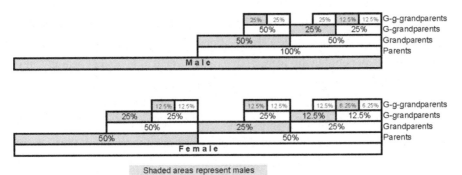

Shaded areas represent males

Figure 0-4

7

The test for the X-chromosome is part of Family Finder. You do not order it on its own.

Note that X-chromosomes are in no way related to MtDNA. Since both of these have a strong female component, some people tend to confuse them.

The testing companies

Family Tree DNA uses a kit for DNA specimens based on a cheek swab. The other companies use spit, which has been a problem with international mail because the kit is considered a medical specimen. Therefore, until recently, only FTDNA has been able to sell kits in many countries outside the United States including Israel.

FTDNA is also the only one of the three companies that offers Y and MtDNA tests.

23andMe originally marketed to people who wanted the medical component of their DNA, and the United States Food and Drug Administration saw that as a problem. Furthermore, because the company was testing people who wanted their own medical data, their customers were far less likely to share their results with their genealogy matches.

Ancestry has consistently refused to provide a chromosome browser, which would enable people to look at their matches on individual chromosomes. Many Ancestry users transferred their results to FTDNA (for a fee) in order to allow proper analysis of matches with the whole range of other customers. The distinct advantage of Ancestry is that their DNA tests are linked to the Ancestry family trees and document database that gives a certain amount of leverage that the other companies do not offer.

My own reason for turning to FTDNA was simpler. My first tests were Y and MtDNA tests, which only FTDNA offers. Furthermore, Family Tree DNA was founded by people who were active in the world of Jewish genealogy, and I felt that the company's approach would be more attuned to my own needs.

And remember, although medication, chemotherapy and the like supposedly do not affect your results, you should rinse out your mouth between eating and testing. You wouldn't want anyone thinking that one of your ancestors was a chicken or a potato.

Chapter One

Immediate and Stunning Results

Joanna

One of the purposes of a family genealogy web site is to serve as a place where family members can discover each other. In the case of the Pikholz Project web site, we occasionally meet a previously unknown branch in exactly this way—someone looks for his grandparent online and finds a mention of the birth on our site.

In June 2011, I received an email from a Polish woman named Joanna in Warsaw telling me that her late maternal grandfather Julian (1911-1986) was the son of a Polish woman and an older Pikholz man. Joanna didn't know the man's first name, but she knew what he did for a living and that he had lived in Klimkowce, a very small town not far from Skalat, near what was then the border between Austrian Galicia and Russia. She continued:

"The features of my grandfather Julian, my mother and her brother, and mine have always been perceived as original and Semitic rather than Slavic, which might be accounted for by our origin and the multicultural mixture existing in the borderland area.

Around the year 2000 my mother told me and my son Filip that my grandfather Julian's father was Pikholtz, the administrator of one of the estates where my great grandmother Marta had worked (she had become a wife and a mother by then, which means that Julian was a child born out of a romance). My mother told us the situation was very awkward. Marta was Julian's lonely mother so, in an intolerant environment, he was badly treated being a child born out of wedlock, and Jewish to top it all.

I took a long time to associate certain facts of my grandfather's life with his speechlessness. Being Polish and Jewish he had to hide from both the Ukrainian Insurgent Army (UPA) and from the Germans. Then he had to hide from the Polish being a Jew. His features and his face were unambiguous.

My mother told us that the Pikholtz family were in the ghetto (probably in Podwołoczyska) during the war. Someone saw the Pikholtz sons being brought away, Julian was said to know one of them personally."

Joanna wanted to know two things—was she a part of the Pikholz family, and did she have living close relatives?

I knew that the estate manager in Klimkowce in that period was Josef Pikholz, the great-grandfather of Jacob Laor. I forwarded Joanna's email to Jacob, and he agreed that we should look into this. Jacob is fluent in Polish, so it was natural that he be Joanna's contact. Joanna was pleased to see the name of Julian's father, as Julian's elder son was Josef, and the family had always wondered why Julian had chosen that name.

If Joanna's story was correct, she and Jacob were half second cousins, sharing a great-grandfather, Josef, but not a great-grandmother. Verifying this seemed to be a perfect use of autosomal DNA.

Autosomal DNA is the genetic material passed down to each child from each parent. This material organizes into two sets of twenty-two chromosomes, one from each parent. The twenty-third pair of chromosomes contains the sex chromosomes, known as X and Y.

The parent passes to the child some mixture of his own two sets of chromosomes received from the grandparents, on average half from each. This means that a child's DNA is composed of roughly one-fourth from each grandparent, but that "one-fourth" is only an average. By the same logic, you can say that a person's DNA is on average one-eighth from each great-grandparent and one-sixteenth from each great-great-grandparent.

Unfortunately, you cannot tell what bits of DNA came from which ancestor. And as the percentages get smaller, some ancestors disappear entirely.

For that reason, autosomal DNA is not reliable beyond the first few generations. In examining a particular ancestry, each subsequent generation is diluted by half due to the introduction of an unrelated "other" parent.

Within the Jewish population, the word "unrelated" is critical. When a set of people have been marrying within a limited pool for hundreds of years, many supposedly unrelated people have, in fact, multiple shared ancestors six or ten or twenty generations previous. This is called endogamy, and it is what makes Jewish genetic genealogy so difficult. Two people can have enough matching DNA to be third cousins, but in fact, they may instead be seventh cousins fifteen times, with splinters of many shared ancestors and individual ancestors shared many times over.

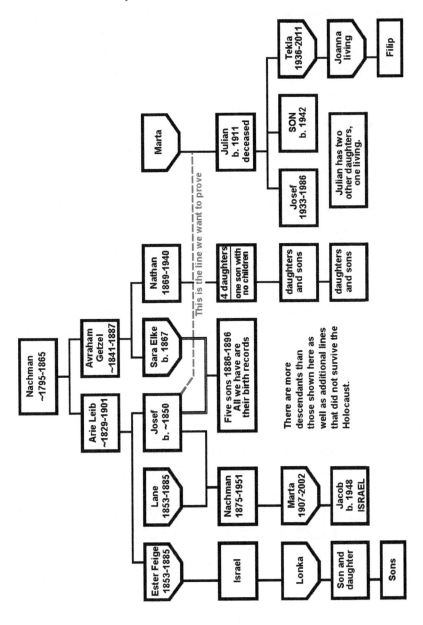

Figure 1-1

The further you get from the shared ancestors, the more these splinters will accumulate, making DNA matching a less reliable test with each generation.

In the case of Jacob and Joanna, this is less of a problem both because they would expect to be relatively close, and because the overwhelming majority of Joanna's ancestors are not known to be Jewish. Joanna's DNA would not be expected to be influenced by any Jewish genetic material other than what she received from their shared great-grandfather Josef.

The Y chromosome

As Jacob and I discussed the idea of autosomal DNA tests for him and Joanna, I pointed out that her uncle Josef would have an unbroken male line from Jacob's third great-grandfather Nachman (~1795-1865). That would mean that Nachman's Y chromosome would have passed down nearly intact all the way to Joanna's uncle Josef. Nachman has no other descendant with an unbroken male line. Perhaps we could use that to confirm what was at once obvious, yet unprovable, that all the Skalat Pikholz families came from a common ancestor.

Joanna's uncle would also be better for the autosomal test than Joanna herself, as he was higher up the ancestral chart. But Joanna's uncle Josef was long dead, and he had no sons to test in his stead. Joanna had a second uncle, one who wanted nothing to do with this Jewish ancestry. She began working on him, promising him above all else that the test would not bear his name.

In the meantime, I looked at the eighteen Skalat families (see Figure i-2) and saw that we had five, aside from Nachman, with living candidates for Y tests. Two of the families who might have been from either Skalat or Rozdol also had unbroken male lines that led to living descendants.

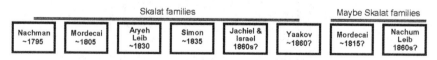

Figure 1-2

Asking these people to do DNA tests and to pay for them as well was not going to be easy. I knew none of them personally. Test candidates in the United States who descended from Aryeh Leib and Simon were on my mailing list, but they rarely responded even to direct questions. Israel had a living grandson here in Israel, but he had no interest in his family background and sent me to his sister, who was none too interested either. Yaakov had two grandsons here in Israel who I thought might be living. Here too, I had brief contact with two of their sisters. Nachum Leib had great-grandsons in the U.S., and yet again, I knew only the sister.

That left the two Mordecais, whom I suspected were the same person. The Mordecai who I knew was from Skalat had one all-male line. I did not know the two third-great-grandsons personally, but I knew their late father's sister Dalia. I knew her and her husband from the years we had both lived in Arad. I was not able to work on genealogy when her mother approached me, but occasionally I would run into Dalia's husband Menachem in the street, and from time to time, I would receive Dalia's parents' mail by mistake. Dalia and Menachem agreed immediately to have one of the nephews do a Y test, and while I was at it, I asked Dalia herself to do an autosomal test.

The other Mordecai was the second great-grandfather of an older man named Vladimir who lived here in Israel. After some difficulties, I had succeeded in making contact with him once, and he told me that his grandfather Yakov had been born in Tulcin in 1878. I had ordered the birth record and learned the name Mordecai from Yakov's father's patronymic.[1]

Other than Dalia, no one responded so I went with what I had. She ordered a Y-37 (that's a Y test with thirty-seven markers) for her nephew Zachy and an autosomal test for herself. As I had ordered my own test a year earlier from Family Tree DNA, we decided to stay with them for these new tests.

Family Tree DNA calls their autosomal test "Family Finder." I decided to do one myself, and while I was at it, I asked my late father's sister Aunt Betty and a first cousin of my father's, Herb, to do Family Finders as well. I have known Aunt Betty well all my life, but Herb and I had met only once when I was fourteen. His parents, Uncle Max and Aunt Mary, had moved from Pittsburgh to Miami before I was born. Herb and I communicated by email, and he was on my genealogy mailing list. He consented to do the test, as did Aunt Betty.

I put together a Hebrew PowerPoint presentation explaining the project and showed it to Dalia and Menachem and to my Galician researcher-friend Dvora Netzer. That became the basis for the presentation I made at the IAJGS Conference in Boston.

With that, we entered the world of DNA testing.

Results from Dalia and Zachy

The family structure (see the chart in the Introduction, Figure i-4) was such that I thought that Dalia's second great-grandfather Mordecai may have been the older brother of my second great-grandmother Rivka Feige, and I referred to Dalia as my fourth cousin.

It was no surprise, therefore, that the results we received from FTDNA called us "suggested third to fifth cousins" and Aunt Betty and Dalia "suggested second to fourth cousins." They had Dalia and Herb a bit closer at "suggested second to third cousins." I attributed that to the fact that Herb and Dalia were Galicianers from both parents, increasing the significance of endogamous connections on their other sides. Herb's non-Pikholz father and Dalia's non-Pikholz mother or grandmother may have had a common ancestor who was influencing these results.

A few weeks later, we received the results of Zachy's Y-37 test. The purpose of that test had been to compare his male line Y-DNA to that of Joanna's uncle. Neither the uncle's tests nor Jacob's had been ordered as yet, but nonetheless Zachy's Y results were stunning. Zachy's Y-37 was a perfect match for my own. My test had been done a year earlier in hopes that we could find some family for my great-great-grandfather, Isak Fischel. Now suddenly he has a surname, and it is Pikholz.

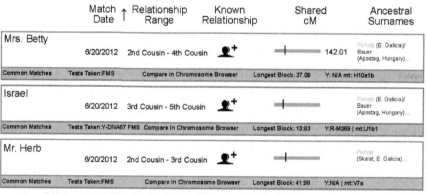

Dalia's original Pikholz matches as they appear on today's match page

Figure 1-3

Since the logic behind my determination that my great-grandfather's mother was a Pikholz remained valid, I could only conclude that my great-grandfather Hersch Pickholz had two Pikholz parents and, that at least on his father's side, Dalia and I have a common Pikholz ancestor.

It also solved a nagging problem that I rarely mentioned. In discussing the family of Mordecai and Taube, I always spoke of Mordecai as the Pikholz even though I knew full well that the Pikholz might have been Taube. The Y match with Zachy made it clear that Mordecai and Izak Fischel both came from a common ancestor.

But now we had a new problem. If I have a double dose of Pikholz DNA from my great-grandfather, Dalia, and I should appear closer than we are. Since we appear as fourth cousins, we must in fact be a bit further than that, probably fifth or even sixth cousins.

The Y match that I have with Zachy does not help on this score. A perfect 37-marker test can tell us we must be related within "genealogical time,"[2] but it cannot be precise. FTDNA says we have a 93 percent chance of being fourth cousins or closer, a 96 percent chance of being fifth cousins or closer, and 97 percent chance of being sixth cousins or closer. I briefly considered upgrading Zachy's test to 67 markers like my own, but if the perfect match remains, it would not make our results more precise.

One thing is certain. The surname of my great-great-grandfather Izak Fischel should definitely be Pikholz, including in the database.

Nonetheless, I cannot "attach" Izak Fischel to Mordecai because I do not know what their relationship is. But I still call Dalia "my fourth cousin."

Results from Joanna and Jacob

It was several months before we actually had tests on order for Joanna and Jacob. While we waited, we proceeded with other tests.

In the meantime, we learned that Jacob's great-grandfather Josef had a grandson on 27 August 1911 named Josef, indicating that Josef was dead by then. Julian was born 16 February 1911 so there is no reason to doubt that Josef is Julian's father.[3]

[1] Tulcin was Russian territory in 1878, so the birth records have the patronymics for both parents. That is different from the Austrian records for Galicia, which have the mother's parents, but no identifying information on the father.

[2] Genealogy researchers use the term "genealogical time" to refer to more recent history; perhaps two or three hundred years depending on place, culture, and level of research. Although we obviously have ancestors going back thousands of years, only the more recent are available according to our current research techniques.

[3] There had been some suggestion that Josef died too early to be Julian's father, and that Julian was fathered by one of Josef's sons. That would have complicated the matter further, as the mother of those sons—i.e. Josef's second wife—was Josef's niece. Therefore, we would have expected Julian to have more Pikholz DNA rather than less. Now that we have the dates, this is no longer a concern.

Chapter Two

"No" is Also an Answer

The Pikholz families of Podolia

Sometimes you think it will be easy, and the actual proof will be only a formality.

Some years ago, I found a death record from Pomona, California, for Nellie Rochester who died 16 May 1931. On her death certificate, her father's name is listed as "? Pickholtz," and her birthplace as "Russia." On her husband's naturalization papers, her birthplace is listed as "Nemerov," which is in Podolia, east of Galicia in the general direction of the port city of Odessa.

I knew the name Nemerov. A few years earlier, I had seen a record of a passenger named Moses Pikholz, age eighteen, from Nemerow sailing from Hamburg in 1891. That would have made him a few years younger than Nellie, who was from the same town. They appear, therefore, to be brother and sister. That is the only reference we have for Moses. We do not even have his arrival at the end of the voyage.

In a 1922 report commissioned by the Odessa Region Committee of Idgezorn published by the American representatives of the All Russian Jewish Social Committee and appearing on *JewishGen*, there is a list of victims of a 1919 pogrom in the town of Tetiev. Among the victims were forty-five year old Hayim Pikholz and three children. We have no other information on this family, but since Tetiev is less than fifty miles from Nemerow, and Hayim is in the same age cohort as Nellie and Moses, it is entirely possible that he is their brother. We have no one else living anywhere near Tetiev.

In Chapter One, I mentioned Yakov the grandfather of Vladimir, who was born 1878 in Tulcin less than 20 miles from Nemerow. Here too we have a possible brother—in this case with names of parents and a grandfather Mordecai.

Research in Podolia is difficult both because it is in Ukraine, and because the archives in Kamenets-Podolsk had burned down in 2003. The few records that were not destroyed were badly damaged by water. Paper records were not going to help, but DNA might.

Of course, Nellie and Moses are more likely to be siblings than Hayim and Yakov since we know they are from the same town.

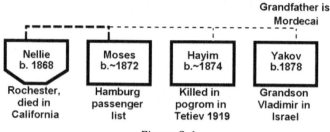

Figure 2-1

Nemerow is about 218 miles from Rozdol but only about 132 miles from Skalat, and it was the Skalaters who began spreading out earlier. So I naturally assumed that the Podolia family—if it was indeed a single family—had come from Skalat.

I have found no descendants of either Moses or Hayim, but we do have descendants of Nellie Rochester. Before they went to California in the early 1920s, Nellie and her husband (then known as Necha and Ruven Rechister) had lived nearly twenty years in Kansas City, Missouri, which is where they were naturalized. Before going to the United States, they had lived in Odessa where some of their children were born. The rest were born in Kansas City.

I had found their children with them in California, but I had never located any living descendants. However, through a newspaper ad I placed in the Kansas City *Jewish Chronicle*, I learned that when they went to California, one married daughter stayed behind. I am in touch with her descendants who are still in Kansas City.

The tests

This looked easy. A Y-37 test can tell if Vladimir's Mordecai might be the same as Dalia's Mordecai. Family Finder autosomal tests for Vladimir and one of Nellie's great-grandchildren in Kansas City should be able to tell us if their late fathers are second cousins of Vladimir. Second cousin once removed is well within the capability of an autosomal test. I ordered a test kit for Vladimir, and Nellie's great-granddaughter Joyce ordered a Family Finder for herself.

Finding Vladimir was no easier the second time than it had been the first time. My researcher-friend, Dvora Netzer, phoned her Russian-speaking Medved cousins who live in the same city as Vladimir, and they set up a meeting for me in their apartment. The Medveds, Vladimir, Dvora, and I met, and we left with two small vials of DNA scraped from the inside of Vladimir's cheek.

I sent Vladimir's sample and Joyce sent hers, and I sat back to wait for the good news.

The results

Nothing at all matched. Vladimir's Y-37 was not close to Zachy's and mine. He had remote autosomal matches with Aunt Betty, Herb, Dalia and later Jacob and Filip. Joyce matched none of them even remotely, not even Vladimir.

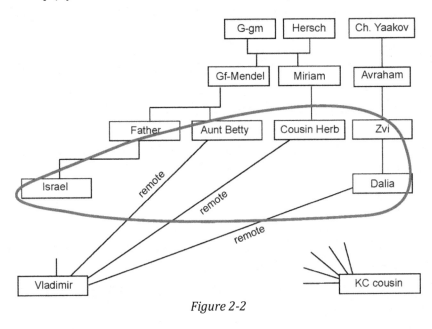

Figure 2-2

Obviously I had it all wrong, but I wasn't sure how. The two families were clearly not closely related, nor were they closely related to those of us who had already tested. Perhaps they were connected to the Rozdol Pikholz families. Or perhaps there was some interruption of the normal transmission of DNA. Children were informally adopted by family members after the death of one or both parents. A child may have been raised by a childless aunt and uncle due to economic issues. A widow who remarried might have the children take on the stepfather's surname. A non-paternal event (NPE)[1] involving hostile neighbors, passing armies, youthful indiscretions or some other behavior that we like to think our ancestors were not susceptible to may have occurred.

Normally when the surname doesn't fit, the default assumption is that the name came from the mother's side as I mentioned in the introduction. Many Jewish marriages in Galicia were never recorded with the civil authorities, so the children were considered illegitimate and given the mother's name even if the father affirmed paternity. But we have the surnames of both of Vladimir's grandfather's parents, so there is not much room for this phenomenon. Joyce's Pikholz genes came from her grandmother and great-grandmother, so here too the non-registered wedding scenario would not fit.

It may be that Joyce is a bit of a DNA outlier among her own family. Her father's brother has four children and they might have a stronger concentration of Pikholz DNA than Joyce.

I hoped if we tested additional Pikholz descendants, we could see where these two Pikholz families fit in with the rest of us. In the meantime, I removed them from the list of Skalaters and added them to the small group of Pikholz families of unclear origin.

Now, more than two years later, I am no closer to a solution. Based on the amounts of matching DNA, Vladimir matches twenty-seven Pikholz descendants none as close as suggested third cousins. Joyce matches sixteen Pikholz descendants, with only one as close as a suggested fourth cousin. I am not willing to declare NPE and disqualify them as genetic Pikholz descendants.

However, I can remove all the "maybe" and "probably" from the comments in both Vladimir's family and the Rochesters from Kansas City. They are definitely not connected in the way I had expected.

I still cannot say one way or the other about Moses from Nemerow and Hayim from Tetiev, and the comments in the database and the website will continue to reflect the uncertainty.

Sometimes you think it will be easy and the actual proof is just a formality. And sometimes you are completely and demonstrably wrong. But this is a DNA success, not a failure. "No" is also an answer.

---

[1] I personally prefer the term "false father" but the genetic genealogy community has settled on "non-paternal event" to describe situations where the father or the paternal line is not what we would have expected.

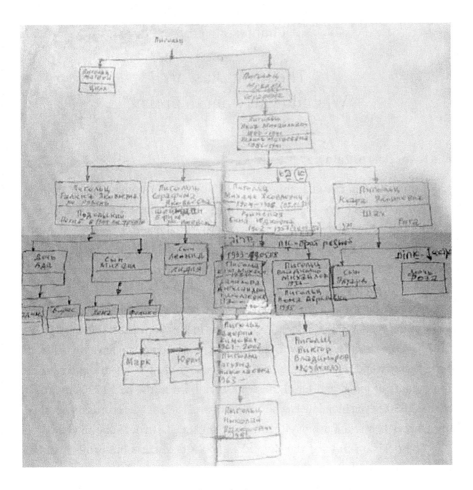

Vladimir's Tree
Figure 2-3

Chapter Three

The Kwoczkas, or
"What do you want to prove?"

The Kwoczkas of Zalosce

I often say that my flagship work is the single-surname Pikholz Project, and that is true as far as it goes. In the course of looking at the records for my grandfather's family in Zalosce as indexed by JRI-Poland, I realized that my great-grandmother's surname, Kwoczka, was nearly unique to this town. There are a few scattered elsewhere, but these are more individuals than families and are probably related to those in Zalosce.

The only birth and death records that AGAD has for pre-1900 Zalosce are 1629 births in the years 1877-1890 and 3314 deaths in the years 1823-1866 and 1877-1897. The surname Kwoczka, with spelling variations, appears in fewer than fifty of these records and as I wrote in the introduction, most of them appear to be descendants of Jossel and Jute Leah who were born in the mid-1790s and died around 1850. Seven individuals who appear in pre-1860 death records do not shed any light on their relationships either to Jossel and Jute Leah or to one another.

The decision to treat the Kwoczkas as a single-surname project was at once obvious and unimportant.

I identified two sons of Jossel and Jute Leah, Mendel (~1825-1896) and Mordecai Meir, my great-great-grandfather. The general structure of the family appears in Figure 3-1.

The box on the lower right shows the seven unattached individuals plus a few Kwoczkas from other towns in the area who are likely part of the Zalosce family.

The problem I had is represented by the broken line in the center identifying Rachmiel as a probable son of my second-great-grandparents Bassie and Mordecai Meir. Rachmiel, who died in 1935 at age seventy-one, is buried in New York, and his tombstone identifies his father as Mordecai without the Meir. On one hand, it would be unusual that the family of a synagogue-attending Jew would not know his father's full name, but the alternative—that Rachmiel's father was some other Mordecai—created problems of its own.

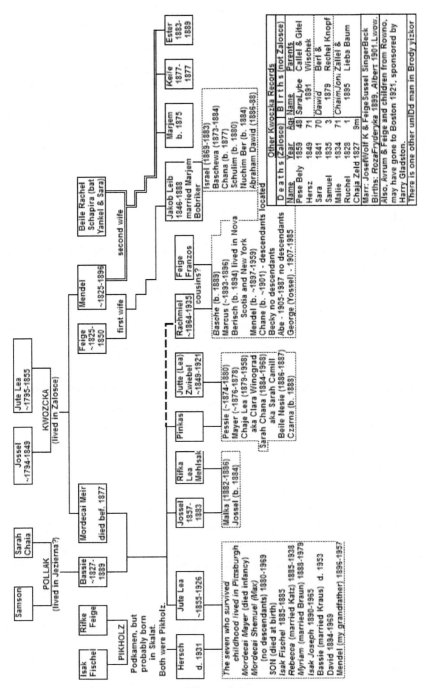

Figure 3-1

23

Mordecai and Mordecai Meir could obviously not have been brothers, so if they were two different people there would have had to be another couple around the same time as Jossel and Jute Leah. There was no indication of such a couple. Aside from that, the names of the children of Rachmiel are consistent with his being the son of Mordecai Meir and Bassie.

Rachmiel had one son named Markus, which in east Galicia was generally Mordecai, who died in December 1896 at age two. But the fact that his death record does not cite a second name is not proof that he didn't have one. The JRI-Poland index does not include a birth record for Markus.

Baruch

I had become friends with Rachmiel's youngest grandson, Baruch, and he could not shed any light on the question. Nor could any of Rachmiel's other descendants with whom I had had brief contact. So the problem remained unsolved, symbolized by the broken line on my chart.

At about the same time as I was trying to organize a Family Finder test with Vladimir's putative cousins in Kansas City (see Chapter Two), I realized that, here too, we had an easy way to prove a relationship. Baruch, whose surname is not Kwoczka despite his being the son of Rachmiel's son, is a second cousin of Aunt Betty and Cousin Herb who had already tested. I asked Baruch to do a Family Finder test and while I was at it, I asked him to do a Y test as well. Jossel Kwoczka (~1794-1849) may have had brothers or cousins with descendants and perhaps we could locate some of the more distant family. Jossel is, after all, my own third great-grandfather.

Baruch, who is a doctor of medicine, asked "What do you want to prove?"

The first part of my explanation was easy. I wanted the Family Finder test in order to see how close a match Baruch is to Aunt Betty and Herb so I could lay to rest the question of one Mordecai or two. Or, in more personal terms, whether Baruch's own great-grandfather was Mordecai or Mordecai Meir. That was a question that he would have no problem accepting as important.

The Y, male line, test was a harder sell. Sometimes you investigate in order to prove or disprove something specific. But sometimes you just want to see what happens. I knew we were at the beginning of what might become a large project, yet only six others had ordered Family Finder tests before Baruch so I really had no idea where we might be going with this. Laying a net to catch some relative of Jossel on his male line who might test years later was not convincing. I did not want to ignore the question entirely; after all, if this project was to grow, it would be a question that would no doubt challenge me frequently.

Baruch agreed to do the Family Finder in order to determine his great-grandfather's full name and to demonstrate the closeness of our relationship. He also agreed to do the Y test, not so much because he thought it useful, but because Jossel Kwoczka was my ancestor, and I had no one else to do the test.

Family Finder Results

Baruch's results came in at the beginning of November 2012, the same day as those for Joyce from Kansas City. FTDNA said he was a "first cousin to third cousin" to both Aunt Betty and Herb. However, both his total match and his largest match segment were both about a third larger for Aunt Betty than for Herb. His match with me, "second cousin to third cousin," was much smaller. This was what we expected, and it settled the question of Rachmiel's father's name, Mordecai Meir. His tombstone is incorrect. The line on the chart was no longer broken.

The test results that came later confirmed this close relationship and, in fact, Baruch's thirteen known cousins are his thirteen closest matches.

There was, nonetheless, a bit of a surprise. Although Baruch is not a Pikholz, he has matches with Vladimir, Dalia, and Joyce. They are remote matches, to be sure, but they are more than what Joyce has with the rest of us.

BARUCH'S MATCHES

	Total match	Largest Segment
Aunt Betty	417.50	86.03
Herb	338.69	62.81
Israel	174.86	24.42
Dalia	69.85	7.84
Vladimir	75.95	13.53
Joyce	64.71	7.71

Figure 3-2

25

The interesting thing here is that Baruch's matches with Dalia, Vladimir, and Joyce are all in the same range, probably due to some distant common ancestors beyond the scope of my research. But Joyce's mother is not Jewish, so Joyce would be expected to show a smaller endogamy effect than the others. This is, of course, a small sample size and not necessarily indicative of anything. I began to think this could be very interesting.

I also had a look at the specifics of the match; that is where these matches are on the chromosomes. If a group of people matches each other in the same place, there is a common ancestor. I had not yet heard of the analytical tool GEDmatch—more about that later—but FTDNA provides a tool called a "chromosome browser" which shows where on each chromosome the matches occur. This tool allows us to look at a person's matches with up to five people at a time to see on which chromosomes the matches appear. The results appear in a colored graphic and an Excel file.

The standard among genetic genealogists calls for three people who match each other on the same segment, but considering our issues of endogamy, I prefer larger groups where possible before drawing conclusions.

Baruch matches Aunt Betty and Herb in seven places on five chromosomes—1, 8, 9, 10 and 15. That to be is expected since they are fairly close relatives with known common ancestors. If any of the others match Baruch in parts of those same places, we would have an indication of a common ancestor for the whole group.

Aunt Betty's matches with Baruch in orange; Herb's matches with Baruch in blue

Figure 3-3

They do not. So far. Dalia, Vladimir, and Joyce have matches with Baruch that are completely different from Aunt Betty and Herb, as well as different from one another. As I would learn in the months that followed, there is a lot of that. It is the effect of endogamy.

Dalia and Joyce each match Baruch on three segments between 6 and 8 centiMorgans (cM).[1] In each case, the three matches could be from one, two, or three common ancestors. The answer to that is probably further back in time than we can go. There are additional matches that are smaller than 5 cM. I will discuss that subject separately in Chapter Ten.

Baruch has one significant match with Vladimir—13.53 cM. This hints at just one common ancestor, possibly less far back. In this instance, testing other relatives might be useful.

To date, Baruch is the only descendant of Rachmiel to test. I would like to have a few more.

There is one other Kwoczka cousin who has tested—Pinchas, a great-grandson of Pinchas Kwoczka, the brother of Baruch's Rachmiel and my Jute Leah. His matches with Baruch do not match Joyce, Vladimir, and Dalia either, which is no surprise.

Y-DNA results

Baruch's Y-DNA test for 37 markers has thus far produced no perfect matches, but he has eleven matches with people with a genetic distance of one. That is, from the time of his common ancestor with these eleven people, there has been one mutation on the thirty seven markers. Statistically it is even money that this common ancestor is only six or seven generations ago.

Only six of those eleven matches have taken Family Finder tests to date. Three of those six are not considered Family Finder matches by FTDNA and the other three appear to be beyond fifth cousins. Of course, this does not mean that some future test will not produce better matches. While expecting short-term success is not realistic, we would like to think that as more and more people take these tests, there will eventually be successful matches.

---

[1] The International Society of Genetic Genealogy (ISOGG) defines a centiMorgan as follows:

"In genetics, a centiMorgan (cM) or map unit (m.u.) is a unit of recombinant frequency which is used to measure genetic distance. It is often used to imply distance along a chromosome and takes into account how often recombination occurs in a region. A region with few cMs

undergoes relatively less recombination. The number of base pairs to which it corresponds varies widely across the genome (different regions of a chromosome have different propensities towards crossover). One centiMorgan corresponds to about 1 million base pairs in humans on average. The centiMorgan is equal to a 1% chance that a market at one genetic locus on a chromosome will be separated from a marker at a second locus due to crossing over in a single generation." (http://www.isogg.org/wiki/Centimorgan)

Or as Kitty Cooper puts it:
You do not need to understand the definition of a centimorgan (cM). Hardly anyone does; just accept that it is the best measure of the importance of a DNA match, the larger the better. (http://blog.kittycooper.com/2015/03/using-your-dna-test-results-the-basics-for-genealogists/)

Chapter Four

Rozdol

Two families or one

The Pikholz Project entered the world of DNA in order to address the specific questions posed by Joanna's story as outlined in Chapter One. This was a Skalat family, and I felt it required a Skalat solution. For this reason, the plan I developed for DNA testing was based only on the Skalat families in my tree and those others who *might* have come from Skalat. The Rozdol Pikholz families were never part of this plan.

South of Lwow, about two thirds of the way to Stryj, Rozdol is smaller than Skalat with fewer Jews and non-Jews alike. *Mapquest* says that the drive from Rozdol to Skalat is two hours and eighteen minutes across the heart of east Galicia along highway M-12, or about thirty minutes longer going via Lwow. I can only guess at how far apart the towns were using modes of travel prevalent in 1800.

While we have documentary evidence of several Pikholz families in Skalat back to the late 1700s, the Rozdol Pikholz families appear to come from a single couple, Pinchas and Sara Rivka who had children in the early 1800s. There was a Pinchas born in 1832 and a Sara Rivka born 1840, so we can assume that the original couple had died by then. Nearly every Pikholz family from Rozdol has descendants named Pinchas or Sara Rivka, often both.

Aside from the unusual and uncommon shared surname, there was never really any reason to think that the Pikholz families from Skalat and Rozdol were, in fact, one family with a common Pikholz ancestor. There was no Pinchas in Skalat and no other significant duplication of given names in the early generations. Although most of the Skalaters lived an Orthodox Jewish lifestyle typical of the day, the Rozdol families appear to have produced more rabbis and other religious functionaries.

Yet I was not willing to rule out the possibility that this was one family living in two distant towns.

Rav Juda Gershon Pikholz (b. 1842), a grandson of Pinchas and Sara Rivka, wrote two books on Jewish law, one of which had significant

29

modifications in a second edition. In those volumes, he offers quite a bit of family information in his introductions and dedications. He refers by name to family members who helped cover publishing expenses, and the text itself is sprinkled with bits and pieces of family information such as "I was asked by my student, my sister's son … Meir Engel from the holy community of Komarno," and the like.

The frontispiece of Rav Juda Gershon's first book
Figure 4-1

Rav Juda Gershon refers to his grandfather as "Pinchas of Rozla" (the Yiddish name for Rozdol), but never as "Pikholz." Reading this, I came to the conclusion that Pinchas was not called Pikholz and that perhaps the surname comes from his wife, Sara Rivka. That could explain why the name Pinchas does not appear in the Skalat families even if we are talking about a single family split between the two towns.

I was also troubled by the geography. I did not understand how a Pikholz woman from Skalat would have married into a family in distant Rozdol.

I saw one possibility that made sense to me. It seems there was a gentile family named Pikholcz who lived in the sub-Carpathian town of Visk, today called Vyskovo. This family was minor Hungarian nobility who had fallen on hard times, and I thought it possible that the Jewish Pikholz families had been tenants of these non-Jewish landowners during the mid or late 1700s. It follows that when required to take surnames, these Jewish tenants may have adopted the surname of the landowner.

The Pikholz family of Rozdol was connected by marriage to the Stegs, in particular the rabbi of Skole, R' Yehudah Zvi Steg. The Stegs had a Hungarian branch, and I began to see a scenario where Sara Rivka of Visk was matched with Pinchas of Rozdol via the Stegs, while the others in her family went from Visk to Skalat. This is, of course, pure speculation on my part.

I had decided to do my research as though the Rozdol and Skalat families were probably not related, but if they were it was through Sara Rivka. In any case, I was going to continue doing the genealogies of both families. But I was certainly not going to mix the Rozdolers into our Pikholz DNA project.

Gary and Amos

Gary decided otherwise. Gary (Gedalyah Zvi) Pickholz is the son of Rabbi Moshe Pickholz, whose great-grandfathers David and Hersch Leib Pikholz are either brothers or first cousins. Gary ordered a Y-37 male-line test, a Family Finder test, and an MtDNA female-line test.

My reaction was to congratulate him on the initiative and to suggest that he be prepared to contact other Rozdol Pikholz descendants and run a DNA project for them. I was not prepared to try to integrate this into my own project for the Skalat Pikholz families, who—I was convinced—were probably unrelated to Gary's Rozdolers.

I did, however, approach Amos and ask him to test. Amos' family is the only one from Rozdol in which the earliest Pikholz ancestor is a woman. I asked him to do both Family Finder and MtDNA tests, which he did.

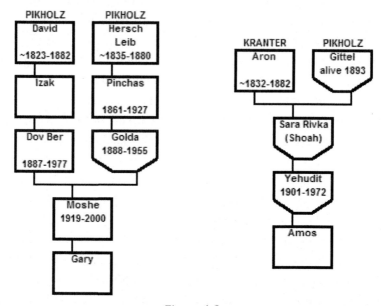

Figure 4-2

Amos' grandmother Sara Rivka had an older brother Pinchas, born in 1859, so her mother Gittel was probably born in the 1830s. That would have made Gittel—as well as Gary's David and Hersch Leib—probable grandchildren of the original Rozdol couple Sara Rivka and Pinchas.

The Family Finder matches show Amos and Gary to be "second cousins-fourth cousins." That seemed reasonable, taking into account the fact that Gary has a double dose of Pikholz DNA from his father's parents.

What surprised me was that Gary matches Herb and Vladimir as "fourth cousin-remote cousin" and Joyce, Aunt Betty and Dalia as "fifth cousins-remote cousins." Amos also matches Joyce and Aunt Betty as "fifth cousins-remote cousins." That is about what I would expect to find for fifth cousins with a common ancestor who had children in the very early 1800s. Perhaps the Skalaters and the Rozdolers were one family after all.

The chromosomes

To examine this more closely, I went to the FTDNA chromosome browser that I described in Chapter Three. If three or four people all match one another in the same place, we can then consider that the segment may have come to all of them from a common ancestor.

Of all the people in the discussion thus far, there is only one such match, on chromosome number 11.

	Start location	End location	cM
	60053455	68173670	7.43
	62596243	68173670	5.49

Figure 4-3

The orange rectangle on the top of Figure 4-3 shows the 7.43 cM match between Amos and Gary. The blue is the smaller match between Aunt Betty and Gary. These are small matches to be sure—not necessarily indicative of a common ancestor in genealogical time, but not to be ignored either.

Of course, even if this is a legitimate ancestral match, we do not know if this indicates a common Pikholz ancestor. It may be from some hitherto unknown common ancestor on Gary's mother's side, Aunt Betty's mother's side and Amos' father's side.

I needed to get more people to test.

Introduction to triangulation

My Kwoczka cousin Baruch (Chapter 3) also matches people he "shouldn't." That's what this endogamy is all about, multiple common ancestors from many directions. Baruch is "fourth cousin-remote cousin" to Vladimir and "fifth cousin-remote cousin" to Gary, Dalia, and Joyce. But what really struck me is that he is a suggested fourth cousin to Amos! That sounds close, all things considered.

I cranked up the chromosome browser once again, this time comparing everyone to Baruch. I found no pattern of matching segments, with one exception. A smallish match on Baruch's chromosome 10 between Gary and Aunt Betty. I did the same thing on Gary's chromosome browser and found that Baruch matches but Aunt Betty does not.

This is triangulation. It is not enough to see that A matches B and C. You also must check separately to see if B matches C. Only then can you ascribe a common ancestor to A, B, and C.

The reason for this is that we have two sets of chromosomes and the FTDNA analysis does not distinguish between them. You cannot tell what you received from your mother and what came from your father.

In this instance, Gary matches Baruch on either Baruch's father's or mother's side, while Aunt Betty matches Baruch at the same bit of chromosome 10 on Baruch's other side. Aunt Betty and Gary do not match each other on chromosome 10.

When I applied this test to the match in Figure 4-3, Gary, Aunt Betty and Amos indeed match each other; so we can conclude that there is a single common ancestor for all three, though not necessarily a Pikholz.

Triangulation is a tool that must be kept close at hand, and I will come back to it in subsequent chapters.

Gary's Y-37 male line test

Then there is the matter of Gary's Y-37 male line test.

Gary is in haplogroup R-M269, which is my own haplogroup. The Wiki page of the International Society of Genetic Genealogists (ISOGG) defines haplogroup as "*a genetic population group of people who share a common ancestor on the patrilineal or matrilineal line.*" But nonetheless, we are not considered a match as nineteen of our thirty-seven markers are not the same.

I never really expected a match here, because as I explained above I believe that if the Rozdol family is part of the Skalat group, it is through Sara Rivka and not through Pinchas. Nonetheless, the male-lines of the Rozdol Pikholz descendants are worth a look on their own merits.

As Figure i-2 in the Introduction shows, there are nine Pikholz families from Rozdol. One is a female line and two others have no male-line descendants. Of the remaining six, three did Y-chromosome tests. Gary and Robert did Y-37 tests, and Micha did the very basic Y-12 test. Micha, who uses the surname of his paternal grandmother, not Pikholz, matches the first twelve markers of Gary and Robert. But Robert and Gary do not quite match each other.

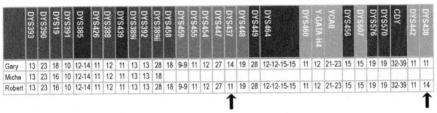

	DYS393	DYS390	DYS19	DYS391	DYS385	DYS426	DYS388	DYS439	DYS389I	DYS392	DYS389II	DYS458	DYS459	DYS455	DYS454	DYS447	DYS437	DYS448	DYS449	DYS464	DYS460	Y-GATA-H4	YCAII	DYS456	DYS607	DYS576	DYS570	CDY	DYS442	DYS438
Gary	13	23	18	10	12-14	11	12	11	13	13	28	18	9-9	11	12	27	14	19	28	12-12-15-15	11	12	21-23	15	15	19	19	32-39	11	11
Micha	13	23	16	10	12-14	11	12	11	13	13	18																			
Robert	13	23	16	10	12-14	11	12	11	13	13	28	18	9-9	11	12	27	11	19	28	12-12-15-15	11	12	21-23	15	15	19	19	32-39	11	14

Figure 4-4

Gary's values for the locations known as DYS437 and DYS438 are 14 and 11 respectively, while Robert's values are the other way around. Since for each of those two locations the difference in values between Robert and Gary is three, the total difference between them is six. That means if their Y comes from a common ancestor, there have been a total of six mutations since that common ancestor. That sounds like way too many for two hundred years. As a comparison, among the three Skalat Pikholz descendants we have zero mutations in more than two hundred years.

It is, of course, possible that the Rozdol male lines do not come from a common ancestor.

The nine known Rozdol lines include David (b. ~1823), Avraham (b. ~1826) and Hersch Leib (b. 1835), all of whose death records name their parents as Isak and Feige Pikholz. There is also a known sister and brother, Sara Rivka and Nachman, whose parents are Isak and Feige; and there is a Pinkas born 1832 to Isak and Feige. All these appear to be siblings, grandchildren of the original Pinchas and Sara Rivka.

See Appendix D for a chart showing the Rozdol Pikholz families.

But it is not that simple. For one, Isak Pikholz is the sandak for the son of Sara Rivka in 1879, but since Sara Rivka had a son Isak born in 1871, this sandak cannot be her father. Her father would not have been alive when she named after him in 1871. Furthermore, we know that David had a son Isak in the 1850s, and he too would not be the grandson of the man with the same name who was living in 1879.

To top it off, we have birth records for Sara Rivka born to Isak and Feige in July 1840 and Sara born to Izig and Feyga in October 1840. It appears, therefore, that there are two contemporaneous couples named Isak and Feige Pikholz in Rozdol, and we have no idea which of the next generation comes from which couple.

Since we begin with the assumption that there is one original couple in Rozdol who had children in the very early 1800s, the most likely possibility is that they had a son Isak who married a Feige and a daughter Feige who married an Isak with both couples using the surname Pikholz.

Non-matching Y chromosomes supports this theory and could help us sort out which lines are from which couple. We know for a start that Robert is a documented male-line fourth great-grandson of the original Pinchas and Sara Rivka of Rozdol.

Gary's male-line is from David, the son of Isak and Feige. His grandmother is from Hersch Leib. Micha is a male-line descendant of Pinkas—perhaps the one born in 1832 to Isak and Feige, but not necessarily. Micha's great-grandfather Pinkas died before 1905, and we do not have Rozdol death records for the early 1900s. The death record for that Pinkas might give his age or his parents' names.

It is also possible that there was an error in the results of either Robert's or Gary's tests, and that in one of the tests the 11 and the 14 were transposed. Even if that were the case, it would not rule out the "two Isak-Feige" scenario.

The FTDNA sale in December gave me the opportunity to upgrade Micha's Y-DNA to thirty-seven markers. If he turned out to match either Robert or Gary, I planned to ask FTDNA to recheck the Y results of the one that did not match. I thought there was a good case for an error on their part.

So it was. Micha's upgraded Y test matched Gary perfectly for thirty-seven markers. I asked the company to recheck Robert's results and it took about an hour for them to determine that there had, indeed, been an error. Robert, Gary, and Micha are identical for thirty-seven markers.

That left three possibilities for the Isak-Feige problem:

1. Isak married Feige and his sister Feige married Isak, and we have no test for a descendant of Feige the sister.

2. Isak married Feige and his sister Feige married Isak, and Isak the son-in-law was a relative with the same Y chromosome as his father-in-law Pinchas.

3. There is only one Isak-Feige couple, and the problems I mentioned above remain unresolved.

Perhaps the three families who have declined to test will change their minds.

There is a lesson to be learned from this exercise—that the company can make mistakes, and that if you can make a decent case they will recheck their data and make corrections if appropriate. But before that can happen, you, the customer, must pay close attention to your results and question what does not make sense. Of course, the other lesson is that if all you have is a single result, you will have no way of knowing if something doesn't make sense. So you have to do as many tests as you can.

At least for now, I have made no commitment regarding the Rozdol and Skalat families. Maybe they are one, maybe they are two. Maybe the DNA matches between them are real Pikholz matches, and maybe they are just endogamy.

Chapter Five

Filip, Jacob, Rita and Others

Filip

When we last heard from Jacob and Joanna (Chapter One), Joanna was trying to convince her uncle to agree to submit a test kit that would serve for both a Family Finder (autosomal) and a Y-37 (male-line) test, promising that she would keep his name out of it. After considerable urging, he agreed to test, and the kit was recorded on Joanna's son Filip's name. I shall refer to this test as though it was done by Filip, even though it is the DNA of his mother's anonymous uncle.

Filip's thirty-seven marker Y-DNA test is a perfect match to Dalia's nephew Zachy and to me, so we know that the three families descend from a common ancestor. Our earliest known Pikholz ancestors were born about 1795, 1805, and 1820. How those three men are related to one another is still a mystery. Based on age alone, Jacob and Filip's Nachman (1795) and my Isak Fischel (~1820) are probably not brothers, while Dalia and Zachy's Mordecai (1805) could be a brother to either or neither.

I took advantage of the Family Tree DNA sale in December 2014 and upgraded Filip's test to sixty-seven markers, which is the same as mine, and we are still a perfect match. This increases the probability that his Nachman and my Isak Fischel are close to a common ancestor. If I had the budget and the motivation, I would probably upgrade Zachy's test as well and perhaps even upgrade all three of us to 111 markers.

We received the Family Finder results for Jacob and Filip in the summer of 2013. FTDNA shows Filip and Jacob to be "suggested second cousins-fourth cousins" but with 54 cM total matching DNA and a largest match of about 25 cM, they appear to be third cousins. That is slightly more distant than I would have liked. Nonetheless, the cousinhood was demonstrated, as was the Pikholz male line, so we welcomed Joanna to the family according to the details she received from her grandmother.

I also looked at the match using the analytical tool *GEDmatch*, a free, online site developed by Curtis Rogers and John Olsen. In addition to providing tools for analysis beyond what the individual testing companies provide, it also allows us to examine matches with people who tested with other companies. Of course, all of this is dependent on our uploading our raw results to GEDmatch.

This can be done anonymously. What I decided to do is to upload our project data, all under my email, and each with an alias that begins with "1Pikholz" and coded to help identification. For example, Aunt Betty's alias is "1Pikholz-SkH-AB" and Gary's is "1Pikholz-Roz-GZP." This allows match results to be sorted so that everyone in our project appears consecutively and anonymously and that family groups can be found easily.

These are the first matches for my sister Amy. The first ones are all known relatives, more or less in the expected order. The small triangles at the top of the columns enable sorting.

			Haplogroup			Autosomal				X-DNA			
List	Select	Sex	Mt	Y	Details	Total cM	largest cM	Gen	Details	Total cM	largest cM	Name	Email
L	□	F	U1b1		A	2715.1	187	1.2	X	196	196	*1Pikholz - SkH - Sj	IsraelP@pi|
L	□	F	U1b1		A	2617.8	180.6	1.2	X	196	196	*1Pikholz - SkH - Ju	IsraelP@pi|
L	□	M	U1b1	R-M269	A	2628	161.1	1.2	X	67.5	67.5	*1Pikholz - SkH - IP	IsraelP@pi|
L	□	F	U1b1		A	2502	167.2	1.3	X	196	196	*1Pikholz - SkH - J	IsraelP@pi|
L	□	M	H10a1b	R-M269	A	2011.8	107.4	1.4	X	100.2	89.8	*1Pikholz - SkH - UB	IsraelP@pi|
L	□	F	H10a1b		A	1871	149.4	1.5	X	60.2	46.5	*1Pikholz - SkH - AB	IsraelP@pi|
L	□	M	H		A	1090.7	104.4	1.9	X	12.3	12.3	*1Pikholz - SkH - ABS	IsraelP@pi|
L	□	F	U1b1		A	1050.9	69.2	1.9	X	80.9	80.9	*1Pikholz - G - K	IsraelP@pi|
L	□	M	V		A	856.4	119	2	X	0	0	*1Pikholz - SkH - HB	IsraelP@pi|
L	□	M			A	823	95.8	2.1	X	0	0	*1Pikholz - G - LSG	IsraelP@pi|
L	□	M			A	394.7	53	2.6	X	16.1	16.1	*1Pikholz - R - Sam	IsraelP@pi|
L	□	U			A	396.7	41.5	2.6	X	0	0	*1Pikholz - SkH - LSS	IsraelP@pi|
L	□	F			A	318.3	45.7	2.7	X	0	0	*1Pikholz - R - BRC	IsraelP@pi|
L	□	F	R0a4		A	331.7	38.6	2.7	X	34.7	15.3	*1Pikholz - G - RPM	IsraelP@pi|
L	□	F			A	236.3	54.8	3	X	0	0	*1Pikholz - SkH - TK	IsraelP@pi|
L	□	M			A	236.1	45.1	3	X	0	0	*1Pikholz - B - Shab	IsraelP@pi|
L	□	M		R-M269	A	212.6	42.4	3	X	0	0	*1Pikholz - SkH - MAI	IsraelP@pi|
L	□	F	N1b2		A	213.5	40.5	3	X	7.6	7.6	*1Pikholz - G - JZJ	IsraelP@pi|
L	□	F			A	177.9	25.1	3.2	X	0	0	*1Pikholz - SkH - Rh	IsraelP@pi|
L	□	M		R-M 269	A	129.4	28.2	3.4	X	0	0	*AIDc	R|
L	□	M	N1b2	J1e	A	134.2	26	3.4	X	0	0	Davic	dc
L	□	M			A	134.2	14.6	3.4	X	9.1	9.1	**JDD	an
L	□	F			A	132.1	14.4	3.4	X	5.2	5.2	Zlata	le|
L	□	M			A	122.4	13	3.4	X	0	0	Walte	ws
L	□	M		E-M35.1	A	108.8	35.3	3.5	X	5.3	5.3	*1Pikholz - Kw - BHF	IsraelP@pi|
L	□	F			A	104.8	21	3.5	X	7.6	7.6	*LindaB	e-b|
L	□	U			A	114.5	16.9	3.5	X	0	0	Jonathan	

Figure 5-1

Matches from GEDmatch are said to be a bit more precise than the matches at the testing companies. Since you can compare many kits at once, I eventually began using GEDmatch for my more serious comparisons whenever possible.

In the case of Jacob and Filip, the GEDmatch "one-to-one" tool shows seven matching segments totaling 51.9 cM. The average for a third cousin relationship[1] is about 53 cM and a fourth cousin about 13 cm. There are two significant segments of 25.6 cMs and 12.2 cMs and four small splinters of less than 5 cMs that are usually not considered significant. The seventh segment is 6.3 cMs that may or may not be significant. I shall discuss that question in Chapter Ten.

Chr	Start Location	End Location	Centimorgans (cM)
1	97242392	98622147	1.0
1	162937879	167209453	6.3
7	80311982	107689456	25.6
11	45032402	56561698	1.7
12	81953928	89091883	3.4
13	58382814	61275050	1.8
19	211912	3720049	12.2

Largest segment = 25.6 cM
Total of segments > 1 cM = 51.9 cM

Figure 5-2

Rita and her cousin

As I mentioned in the introduction, Rita posted on *JewishGen* in August 1998 looking for traces of her grandmother's brother Shoil Pikholz. He had been up in years when he left Galicia for "Palestine" after WWI, but no one knew what became of him. We still don't.

Rita's own knowledge went back to her great-grandfather Ari Leib Pikholz and included a number of her grandmother's cousins. Much of the family lived in Kozowka (a suburb of Kozowa) and Proszowa.

At the time, we did not know the name of the patriarch who tied all these cousins together, but eventually we determined that his name was Moshe Hersch, born probably around 1825 in Skalat. His wife was Bassie, and both names appear in subsequent generations. The name Nachman also appears in later generations, which brought me to consider that Moshe Hersch might be a son of Jacob and Filip's Nachman who died in 1865 at age seventy. This was reinforced by a Getzel Pikholz from Kozowka—a name that also appears among Nachman's sons. I began referring to the families with these uncommon given names as "the Nachman-Getzel group," believing these names indicated a recent common ancestor, most likely the Nachman who was born about 1795.

Rita had done a Family Finder test about the same time as Jacob and Filip. Her match with Jacob was consistent with fourth cousin, which is what would be correct if her Moshe Hersch was indeed the son of Jacob's Nachman. Rita did not, however, have any significant matches with Filip and the two small ones she had were not shared with Jacob.

Rita's other Pikholz matches caught me by surprise. Remember, I was new to this game and still hoped that everything would fall neatly into place. Rita matches me as a "fourth cousin- remote cousin" but does not match Aunt Betty or Cousin Herb, who should be better matches than me. She matches the mysterious Vladimir remotely, but not Dalia at all. And she has remote matches with Gary and Amos from Rozdol and three other Rozdolers I have not yet introduced to you, the reader. There is no pattern to the chromosome segments that would indicate any path to common ancestry. It is just these splinters of our more distant ancestors, splinters of DNA that remind us that we are in the end, one people, all related. Endogamy.

To clarify the connection between Rita's family and Jacob's, we needed some additional tests. A Y test in Rita's family is not possible as all the surviving families have daughtered out. There are no living males who would carry Moshe Hersch's Y chromosome.

Nor is there much diversity among the candidates for a Family Finder test. Rita's grandmother had a sister with two granddaughters, second cousins of Rita—one of whom I had actually met—but they declined to test. There was another second cousin, Roslyn, who agreed. Roslyn's grandparents were first cousins, both grandchildren of Moshe Hersch. If Roslyn didn't give us much diversity, at least she had a double dose of Pikholz DNA that gave her the "DNA value" of someone in her mother's generation.

Roslyn matches Rita as an estimated "first cousin-second cousin" which is correct and Jacob as a "second cousin-fourth cousin" as expected. Her match with Filip is "fifth cousin-remote cousin." The bad news is that on her chromosome browser there are no overlapping matches. Roslyn matches Rita, Jacob, and Filip as though those three are not related to one another. The good news is that Roslyn has better matches with the other Skalat Pikholz tests than Rita does.

I am still quite sure that this is one family and that Rita's Moshe Hersch is the son of Jacob and Filip's Nachman, but I'd like to see better DNA matches.

Fortunately, FTDNA, as I mentioned above, had a huge sale in December 2014. Among the two dozen Pikholz descendants who ordered Family Finder tests, two are from Jacob's family. One is a descendant of Josef's sister Ester Feige, and one is a descendant of Old Nachman's son Avraham Getzel.

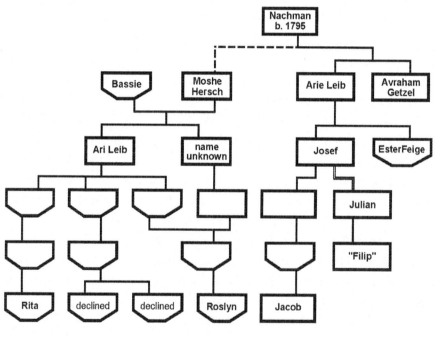

Figure 5-3

Susan and Maciej

It was late April 2015 by the time we had results for Jacob's known cousins Susan and Maciej (pronounced "Matz-ye.") Susan is in the same generation as Jacob, Rita, and Roslyn, while Maciej is one generation younger.

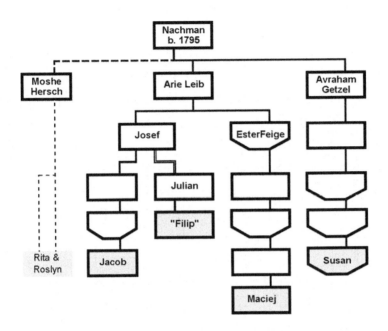

Figure 5-4

The results from FTDNA were not pretty. Neither is considered a match with Jacob. Maciej and Filip are suggested second-fourth cousins, but other than that, I did not see the quality of matches that I would have liked. So I had a look at the one-to-one matches on GEDmatch.

The results are in Figure 5-5, with the FTDNA results tacked on at the bottom of each one.

Jacob's matches with both Susan and Maciej are above 55 cM. Neither match has a segment as large as 9 cM, nonetheless 50 cM puts them in the third cousin range, which is near where they should be. Susan and Roslyn—fourth-remote cousins according to FTDNA—have matches totaling 75.4 cM with a segment of 11.4 cM and another of 9.1 cM. The match between Maciej and Filip is only 68 cM total, but it features a large segment of 27.3 cM.

The "no match" between Maciej and Roslyn also exceeds 50 cM.

Since most of the matching segments are small, there are not large or medium sized segments with groups of the kits. As we shall see in subsequent chapters, we could have better matches at the fourth cousin level, but the level we have here is not outside the norm.

Maciej and Rita

Chr	Start Location	End Location	cM
2	205597847	210509508	5.5
10	102259075	108101115	3.4
11	79583074	82528144	2.5
12	112072514	114682597	5.1
13	77579206	84713786	5.3
14	62133750	68360061	4.2
15	45944278	51558139	3.8
17	46223072	52100338	7.5

Largest segment = 7.5 cM
Total of segments > 1 cM = 37.1 cM

FTDNA: Fifth-remote cousins

Maciej and Roslyn

Chr	Start Location	End Location	cM
1	41177183	45216625	3.2
2	53209267	56490033	2.3
3	8298456	11093817	5.9
3	189810377	193334986	8.1
6	31619117	32908733	1.2
7	22121974	24933115	3.0
8	70368717	73415432	5.4
15	46039413	52099475	4.3
15	68079764	77149214	8.1
19	2868612	5677827	10.1

Largest segment = 10.1 cM
Total of segments > 1 cM = 51.6 cM

FTDNA: No match

Maciej and Filip

Chr	Start Location	End Location	cM
1	33701345	58566605	27.3
1	183334428	191157671	4.9
2	51165036	53489828	1.5
3	163519401	167747794	2.3
3	128385469	131845983	2.6
5	42558929	52878326	2.5
5	55448597	57951028	2.8
6	27359358	32484724	1.3
6	85035960	95159122	8.6
7	51816972	54675550	1.8
14	40229548	44155177	2.4
20	51803451	55729118	10.0

Largest segment = 27.3 cM
Total of segments > 1 cM = 68.0 cM

FTDNA: Second-fourth cousins

Maciej and Jacob

Chr	Start Location	End Location	cM
3	46125404	54572869	3.9
3	189810377	193568785	8.6
6	115089349	121832689	2.8
8	78807160	83952022	3.6
8	110164809	116237586	1.9
9	22819231	26703335	4.6
11	62643376	66537839	3.3
13	66633987	72068378	5.4
13	97310047	99292738	3.0
13	109299721	116251198	7.2
14	70820873	74072360	3.6
14	76030155	78975479	4.1
20	729645	2424631	5.0

Largest segment = 8.6 cM
Total of segments > 1 cM = 56.9 cM

FTDNA: No match

Susan and Rita

Chr	Start Location	End Location	cM
1	20638866	23870723	4.7
3	36468677	40885631	3.5
3	144909730	148455779	2.9
4	166259824	170295694	4.1
5	5330095	7634983	5.6
5	111576733	115378433	3.5
6	85164475	88992471	1.4
8	22840680	25286085	3.0
11	82228035	87828341	4.2
11	90885957	94953939	3.5
18	20927234	23021484	3.5
20	44993134	48117845	6.3

Largest segment = 6.3 cM
Total of segments > 1 cM = 45.9 cM

FTDNA: No match

Susan and Roslyn

Chr	Start Location	End Location	cM
1	1487687	4269934	9.1
2	183154203	189006561	2.6
3	128171249	131501046	2.7
4	12778042	15600113	4.3
6	28556873	36736020	5.3
6	42018042	44735522	6.1
6	150718409	153796006	5.7
7	85411596	88757329	1.7
8	79922054	84902684	3.6
9	94823293	100153062	4.1
13	21641154	26267683	11.4
14	23728397	29110005	6.9
16	12523670	16142100	5.3
18	14725684	22319667	6.6

Largest segment = 11.4 cM
Total of segments > 1 cM = 75.4 cM

FTDNA: Fourth-remote cousins

Susan and Filip

Chr	Start Location	End Location	cM
1	25226290	31856062	8.1
1	47367522	52818028	2.6
1	151671432	159112908	11.1
1	182335838	191076790	5.6
2	212128005	215712179	3.7
9	97077293	101335506	3.3
12	207776581	22224991	2.3
14	91716795	94315023	4.7

Largest segment = 11.1 cM
Total of segments > 1 cM = 41.4 cM

FTDNA: Fifth-remote cousins

Susan and Jacob

Chr	Start Location	End Location	cM
1	162878525	165666127	3.6
2	155099251	162493569	5.8
4	77562172	81379871	3.1
6	31652204	32794081	1.1
7	96882641	101335506	3.5
9	43700096	7520883	5.7
11	38474517	44883396	6.1
13	72684792	74937377	4.1
13	107046046	109664266	7.9
14	62850476	71086366	7.4
18	38045231	41266003	2.0
19	8575931	12522178	6.9

Largest segment = 7.9 cM
Total of segments > 1 cM = 57.2 cM

FTDNA: No match

Figure 5-5

44

I am prepared to say that Moshe Hersch is a son of Old Nachman, notwithstanding some of the weak matches. But if I had the opportunity to ask additional members of both families to do Family Finder tests, I would.

---

[1] A table showing the average number of cM for each relationship and the amount of autosomal DNA shared by people according to relationship can be found on the ISOCC wiki at http://www.isogg.org/wiki/Autosomal_DNA_statistics.

Chapter Six

Moshe Hersch

Rita's great-great-grandfather is not the only Moshe Hersch Pikholz in Skalat in the early 1800s. There are, in various documents, references to three others. There are also two references to people named Moshe who may or may not have an unrecorded second name.

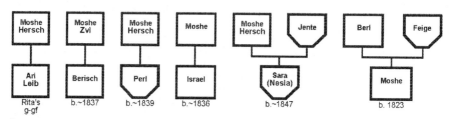

Figure 6-1

Other Pre-1830 Skalaters named Moshe Hersch Pikholz

Berisch Pickholtz went from Skalat to Odessa and then in 1890 to the United States. His wife Sara Bernstein, also from Skalat, died in 1892 and Berisch married her sister Bluma, adopting (whether formally or informally, no one knows) her teenage son Moshe Hersch Werfel who took the name Harry Pickholtz. I consider the name of the son to be coincidence, not relevant to our Moshe Hersch question.

On Berisch's Philadelphia tombstone he is called "Dov Ber ben Moshe Zvi," Zvi being Hebrew for the Yiddish name Hersch. According to his American records, Berisch—or Bernard as he was known—was born about 1837. Using a well-known rule of thumb of Jewish genealogy for that period that a man's first child was born when he was twenty-five (twenty-two for first-time mothers), Moshe Hersch would have been born about 1812 if Berisch was indeed his first child. Berisch's mother's name is not recorded.

There is a Skalat death record for three year old Perl Pikholz on 27 December 1842 with the father named as Moshe Hersch. The mother's name is not mentioned. This Perl could easily be a sister of Berisch, but need not be.

There is a Skalat death record for seven year old Israel Pikholz on 17 January 1843 with the father named as Moshe Pikholz. The mother's name is not mentioned here either.

There is a Skalat death for Sara Pikholz, the wife of Szulim Pikholz, on 28 June 1887 at age forty. According to the birth records for three of her children, Sara's father is Moshe Hersch Pikholz and for two of the three the mother's name Jente appears. On some of the births, Sara is called "Sara Nesia."

There is one other Moses Pikholz from the same period. According to his (long after the fact) marriage record, he was born in 1823 and his parents are Berl and Feige. I do not believe he has anything to do with any of the others mentioned above. We cannot confirm any living descendants of Berl and Feige.

None of those mentioned here appear to have anything to do with Rita's great-great-grandfather Moshe Hersch who I discussed in Chapter Five, though they could certainly carry the name of a common ancestor.

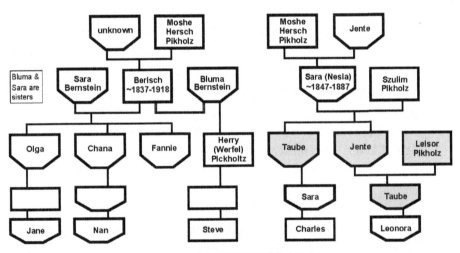

The names shaded in grey have two Pikholz parents.

Figure 6-2

The two questions are:

1. Are Moshe Hersch the father of Berisch, and Moshe Hersch, the father of Sara, the same person?

2. If so, is Jente the mother of both or might Berisch's mother be someone else?

I am ignoring the question of the two children Perl and Israel. The best I can say is that if the two people named Moshe Hersch are the same person, then those two children are probably his.

Researchers are hampered in this period by a lack of records. There are no Skalat birth records at all before 1859, and there are death records only through 1845 and again from 1859. There could, therefore, be additional children I don't know about.

There is no candidate for a Y male-line test as the existing lines are daughtered out.

The potential for genetic testing

There are several descendants who agreed to do Family Finder tests. Jane and Nan are great-granddaughters of Berisch from two of his daughters. Fannie had no children. Charles and Leonora are great-grandchildren of Sara from her two daughters. Sara had four other children who died in childhood.

Steve Pickholtz also tested even though he does not appear to have any Pikholz DNA himself. He is, however, a third cousin of Nan and Jane by virtue of their great-grandmothers being Bernstein sisters, and that allows me to see that some segments of Jane and Nan's shared DNA is from the Bernstein side, not the Pikholz side.

It also gives me the opportunity to mention that Steve, despite not being a genetic Pikholz, is the most active of the Americans in our Pikholz research. Among other things, he is responsible for bringing Jane and Nan into the discussion.

It is possible that Steve has Pikholz DNA from a more distant generation, as is the case with anyone else from the Skalat area. Nan has Pikholz DNA on her mother's side and normal Jewish DNA from her father's side, which may affect her test results. Jane has Jewish DNA only on her father's side, so there is less endogamy in her results.

Nan's son and daughter also did Family Finder tests, but since I have Nan's results, I am not taking them into account. They have Pikholz matches that Nan doesn't, so apparently their father has some obscure Pikholz ancestry.

Charles' grandmother has two Pikholz parents, hence a double dose of Pikholz DNA. Leonora's mother who was born in Skalat has four Pikholz grandparents and at least five Pikholz great-grandparents, so her DNA is heavily influenced by the Skalat Pikholz families. On the other hand, Leonora's father is Central Asian with no Jewish DNA whatsoever. Because of the high concentration of Pikholz DNA, I should probably add Leonora's sister to the mix when I have the opportunity.

Jane's test results

One of the great frustrations over the years of work on the Pikholz Project—both for me personally and for the descendants of Berisch Pikholz—is that we have learned very little about that family. I developed and discarded a few theories about who he might be—other than the son of someone called Moshe Hersch—and we remained stymied. When Jane tested in 2013, I had hoped that her matches within the Pikholz families would show some kind of pattern.

FTDNA declared Jane to be a second cousin-fourth cousin to my father's cousin Herb and to me, as well as to Rita's cousin Roslyn.

They called her a third cousin-fifth cousin to Dalia and to Dalia's third cousin once removed Lloyd, my second cousin Terry, and two Rozdolers. Later my second cousin Rhoda joined that list.

Among the more remote matches were Aunt Betty, Uncle Bob, my second cousin Lee, my third cousin once removed Ralph, some more Rozdolers, and Vladimir.

The no-shows, who are not even remote, include two of my sisters Amy and Sarajoy; the trio Jacob, Filip and Rita; and Joyce from Kansas City.

I looked at Jane's individual chromosomes and found five of interest, by virtue of both their multiple matches and the very long segments.

Note that on the chromosome browsers provided by both FTDNA and GEDmatch, the bars that represent the matching segments are not proportional. Longer bars can represent shorter segments and vice versa.

On chromosome 1, Herb and Rhoda match Jane with identical segments of nearly 43 cM, and Ralph matches over 41 cM on the same segment. Also on the same segment, Terry has over 25 cM, and I have nearly 20 cM. Aunt Betty and Vladimir have smaller matches in the same segment. This indicates that both Jane and my personal family inherited that segment from a common ancestor.

Another nice match between Jane and parts of my family is on chromosome 14, where Aunt Betty and Lee match Jane on an identical 14.5 cM segment, and I match there in a slightly longer segment. Great care is required here because the match could be on my grandmother's side and not on my Pikholz side, as Lee is a double second cousin. (See Appendix B.)

On chromosome 20, Jane has a matching segment of 41 cM with Lloyd but not with anyone else and a 31 cM matching segment with Dalia that includes nearly 15 cM with Lloyd. I am not sure about the larger match with Lloyd, but the one that includes Lloyd and Dalia is definitely of interest. Perhaps Jane's Moshe Hersch and Dalia's great-great-grandfather Mordecai are brothers.

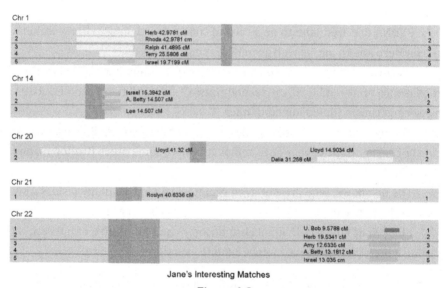

Jane's Interesting Matches

Figure 6-3

On chromosome 21, Jane has a segment of over 40 cM with Roslyn, which should indicate a common ancestor with Old Nachman. But I'd feel better about this one if Jane matched Jacob, Filip, or at least Rita.

Finally, on chromosome 22, Herb has a 19.5 cM match with Jane that includes segments of over 13 cM that match with Aunt Betty, Amy and me, plus one of nearly 10 cM with Uncle Bob. Herb is not on my grandmother's side, so this is more clearly a Pikholz match than the one chromosome 14.

This may be telling us that Jane's Moshe Hersch is a brother to both Dalia's Mordecai and my Isak Fischel. But perhaps not. At that genetic distance, it's hard to tell if we have two brothers, two cousins or an uncle and a nephew.

The other test results

If the two people named Moshe Hersch Pikholz are the same man, Nan and Jane are third cousins to Charles and Leonora. The two men named Moshe Hersch cannot be brothers since they have the same name. If they are not the same man, Nan and Jane are further than fourth cousins to Charles and Leonora. Furthermore, if Berisch and Sara have the same father but different mothers, Nan and Jane would only be half-third cousins to Charles and Leonora.

When results came in for Leonora, Charles and Nan, the three appeared as a very tight group, with Jane not far off. They are right in the middle of the suggested ranges, with Nan closer to Charles and Leonora than expected.

At this level, endogamy should not do much to distort the predictions. The ISOGG wiki says that first cousins share about 850 cM, second cousins about 212 cM and third cousins about 53 cM. It would take a very large number of seventh and eighth cousin matches to bump someone from one of those categories to another.

		Total cM / Longest cM				Ranking			
		Charles	Leonora	Jane	Nan	C	L	J	N
Suggested relationship	Charles	X	291/44	123/26	276/29	▬	1	15	2
	Leonora	1-3 cousins	X	116/26	162/35	1	▬	8	3
	Jane	2-4 cousin	2-4 cousin	X	322/57	6	5	▬	1
	Nan	1-3 cousin	2-3 cousin	1-3 cousin	X	2	3	1*	▬

*The rankings for Nan do not include her children, who are first and second

Figure 6-4

But I wanted to be sure, so I looked at the chromosomes. I did comparisons on GEDmatch of Charles, Leonora, Nan, and Jane to one another and noted the matches of 10 cM or more plus the smaller matches on those same segments. I do not mean to imply that I think that matching segments smaller than 10 cM are not significant. They certainly can be. But I don't think I need them to do this particular analysis. In any case, when using DNA to make a case about someone born two hundred years ago, I prefer to be conservative especially since Charles and Leonora have multiple Pikholz ancestors.

Figure 6-5 shows the results. Let's look at them.

Chr.	Known second cousins						Suggested third cousins											
	Charles and Leonora			Jane and Nan			Charles and Nan			Charles and Jane			Leonora and Nan			Leonora and Jane		
	Start	End	cM	Start	End	cM	Start	End	cM	Start	End	cM	Start	End	cM	Start	End	cM
1 T				72,728,826	94,269,255	19.3												
1 T				119,947,406	162,773,132	23.9												
1 X				207,823,042	234,245,665	31.1												
2	8,874	6,311,894	12.3				62,483,871	68,271,797	5.6	8,874	3,941,740	6.5	82,482,882	68,178,083	5.5	8,874	5,174,807	10.1
2	37,622,471	79,332,496	42.8										176,993,163	185,496,245	9.9			
3				181,171,298	187,880,168	10.5												
4	88,870,120	104,229,478	12.6															
6	108,963,071	132,291,834	18.1										71,768,268	98,183,749	17.0			
8				31,139,701	57,829,780	16.0	70,750,837	99,398,781	23.7									
8				9,477,652	80,245,388	53.6												
8																		
9																		
10 T	80,737,046	85,475,453	5.3				80,489,138	88,568,658	8.1				80,882,517	85,696,328	5.3			
11	23,472,280	61,542,114	28.5				188,510	12,982,874	28.5									
11							126,943,151	132,130,878	14.7									
11																		
12	61,880	6,817,341	18.6															
12	7,982,082	24,820,709	27.0															
14							78,279,942	89,932,491	13.6	31,284,891	65,609,548	27.9				18,397,823	28,783,785	22.1
14																77,744,011	89,966,931	14.3
15	24,230,205	34,002,036	23.2				66,985,678	89,617,776	27.6									
16				27,087,024	57,244,669	23.2	31,284,891	57,503,185	20.0									
17 T							41,740,882	87,380,279	26.3									
18																		
20 T2	2,978,832	6,261,621	10.1	9,236,522	18,912,360	18.3	9,300,254	16,223,638	13.9	1,920,460	16,333,323	34.1				60,321,708	74,860,725	32.2
20 T?				31,943,651	62,326,876	60.0	42,447,380	49,368,646	10.3	42,489,978	47,874,280	9.8				2,978,832	6,266,169	10.2
22	32,634,073	43,492,082	18.1										46,622,891	57,567,536	24.5	46,622,891	57,567,536	24.5

Figure 6-5

There are two matches on chromosome 2. The first involves Charles, Leonora, and Jane, each matching the other two on a segment that is at least 6.5 cM. For two of the three matches, the matching segment is longer. A second match on the same chromosome includes Charles, Leonora, and Nan. The match between Charles and Leonora is 42.8 cM, and Nan matches about 5.5 cM of that with each. Both of these are acceptable triangulation, though not particularly exciting.

Another successful small triangulation appears on chromosome 10, with Charles, Leonora, and Nan.

There is a larger set of three matches on chromosome 16, where Jane and Nan match (23.2 cM). Charles and Nan match (20 cM), and Charles and Jane match (27.9 cM). This is considered proper triangulation and more persuasive than the smaller matches on chromosomes 2 and 10.

Chromosome 3 is different. Nan and Jane have a match of 10.5 cM, and Leonora and Nan have 9.9 cM in the same place. However, Jane and Leonora do not match there at all, so here the test of triangulation fails to prove a match among the three. Jane and Leonora each match Nan but not each other, so the only conclusion can be that one matches Nan on her father's side and the other on her mother's side.

Chromosome 20 has an interesting match of 34.1 cM between Charles and Jane. Within that segment, both match Leonora (about 10 cM each) in the same place and both match Nan in a different place (18.3 cM and 13.9 cM). These five overlapping segments give us two more good-sized triangulations.

Also on chromosome 20, Jane and Nan have a 60 cM match, which includes a segment where both match Charles (about 10 cM) and another where both match Leonora (24.5 cM) precisely. This is different from the previous pair of matches because here there is an overlap between the two.

Jane & Nan
Jane & Charles
Jane & Leonora

Figure 6-6

Twenty-three percent of Charles' match with Jane overlaps with Leonora's match with Jane. Since Nan's match with Jane covers both the others, Charles must match Leonora on that small segment. I discussed this with blogger Roberta Estes (*dna-explained.com*) who suggested that I should lower the threshold so that smaller segments would show up. When I did that I saw that both Charles and Leonora had a few small segments that if connected would show Charles and Leonora matching Jane and Nan and also each other for nearly the entire length of their two segments shown in Figure 6-6.

This shows the importance of small segments, a subject which I shall discuss at greater length in Chapter Ten. However, we have enough unambiguous matches within this group that we needn't depend on the "small segments" argument for chromosome 20.

On other chromosomes there are six one-on-one matches between Charles and Nan, four of them more than 23 cM; three between Leonora and Jane (32.2, 22.1 and 14.3 cM); and one of 17 cM between Leonora and Nan. I have not counted these as they may be from another unknown ancestor, but they lend support to the idea that the two sets of second cousins are third cousins to one another.

That would confirm that the two great-great-grandfathers named Moshe Hersch are the same man and that he was also the father of Perl and probably Israel. In my database and website, I shall record Perl as a full sister of Berisch. Because his father is called "Moshe" without "Hersch," I shall leave Israel undefined but with a comment that he may be from the same family.

We may have enough matching DNA to say that the wife of Moshe Hersch was Jente in both cases rather than his having had two wives, but I will take the conservative decision to record that as "probably."

Chapter Seven

Uncle Selig and the Traffic Light

About forty years ago when I was collecting genealogy rather than doing actual research, my father made his only contribution to the family history telling me that a) his grandfather Hersch Pickholtz had a brother Jachiel, and b) Hersch Pickholtz had an uncle, Selig Pickholtz, who lived in the same area.

My father's grandfather died when my father was eight years old, so my father never really had significant conversation with him. My father had no recollection of how he happened to pick up this bit of information about Uncle Selig. Surely, Hersch had other aunts and uncles. What was significant about this uncle that he was mentioned? Even Cousin Herb, who is four years older than my father, had never heard of Uncle Selig—and his grandfather Hersch had lived with Herb's parents for a time while Herb was growing up.

As I explained in the introduction, traditional genealogy brought me to the following structure with the broken line connecting Selig and Rivka Feige as my father's contribution, and the connection of those two to Isak Josef as my own surmise.

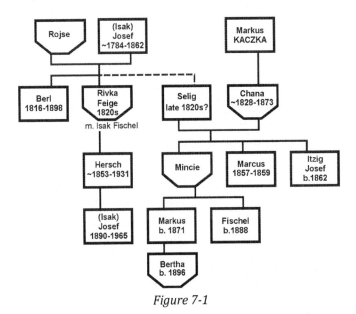

Figure 7-1

I thought that was as far as I would ever get, though the fact that we had marriages for Mincie's sons Markus and Fischel gave me some hope. Bertha's 1896 birth records appeared in the All Galicia Database[1] in 2013, and that added to my optimism.

Uncle Selig in 1911

We next see Selig Pickholz—and this is a unique name, so there is little danger of its being someone other than Uncle Selig—in a typewritten document from 8 July 1929 in Tarnopol. That document is a version of a handwritten birth record for one Dawid Eisig, the son of Salomon Lippman and Gittel, the daughter of Josef and Sussel Pickholz.

O_d_p_i_s_.

Rzeczpospolita Polska. Wojewódstwo tarnopolskie.Starostwo Tarnopol. L.p. 55o/29 opłata stemplowa 1 zloty. Ś w i a d e c t w o u r o- d z e n ia.Wyciąg z metrykalnej księgi urodzonych metrykalnego okrę- gu Tarnopol. Tom 43 Stronica 18. 1. Liczba porządkowa 86.2.Urodze- nia.Dzień - 18 - Miesiąc lutego.Rok 1911. Miejsce i No.domu Gaje wielkie. 3. Obrzezania lub nadania imienia. Dzień, miesiąc,rok -25- lutego 1911 - Miejsce i No domu Gaje wielkie. 4. Imię:Dąwid Eisig Dziecięcia Płeć żeńska lub męska męska. 5. Urodzenie ślubne rzekome, ślubne lub nieślubne : ślubne. 6. Imię i nazwisko ojca jakoteż jego stan, zatrudnienie i miejsce zamieszkania Salomon Lippman kupiec w Podhajcach. 7. Imię i nazwisko matki, jej stan i zamieszkanie,ja- koteż imię i nazwisko, zatrudnienie i miejsce zamieszk.jej rodzi- ców Gittel, zam: córka małżonków Józefa i Süssli Pickholz. 8.Własno- ręczny podpis z wymienieniem zatrudnienia i miejsca zamieszkania kumów lub świadków sandeka lub szamesa Selig Pickholz 9.obrzezu-

Figure 7-2

The birth was 18 February 1911, the circumcision and naming took place on the eighth day, and the sandak[2] was Selig Pickholz. The typewritten document, when Dawid Eisig was eighteen, had something to do with his matriculation or acceptance to higher education. Both documents were in the possession of Dawid's son, whose name is also David.

Uncle Selig had a son in 1857 and a brother born 1816, so I assumed he himself was born in the late 1820s, perhaps very early 1830s. In any event, in 1911 he was almost certainly at least eighty years old.

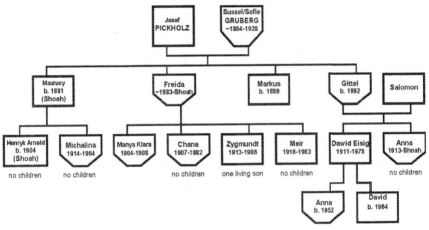

Figure 7-3

I knew the family of Josef and Sussel fairly well, initially from vital records, Holocaust records, and a few graves here in Israel. I also knew the grave of the grandmother Sussel in Karlsbad that someone found and photographed when they happened to see it and thought of me. Such is genealogy when you have an unusual and uncommon surname.

I had been corresponding with David for a couple of years, and he had even taken a Family Finder test that had fewer matches than most. That was not remarkable as his mother is not Jewish, and so does not suffer significantly from Jewish endogamy. I had actually met David's half-sister Anna when I was in Washington, D.C. in 2011.

I had also had some brief correspondence with David's second cousin, the son of Zygmundt, who lives here in Israel. He told me that his father had a sister Chana and had helped me locate Michalina's grave. Michalina, using her partisan name Olga Barnitsch, had submitted a lengthy testimony about her Holocaust experiences and named some of her family.

But the name that stood out in this family was the grandfather Josef. I knew nothing about him except that he was old enough to have a son (Maurycy) in 1881. Could he be Itzig Josef, the son born to Selig and Chana in 1862?

Haus-Nr.	Monat und Tag	Namen des Kindes	Geschlecht				Namen		
			ehelich		unehe-lich		des Vaters	der Mutter	der Mutter-Vater
			männlich	weiblich	männlich	weiblich			
60	10	Itzig Joseph Pick Moses Chajm	1				Selig	Chane	Marcus Kaczka
200	14	Rosenfeld	1				Isaac	Alte	

Figure 7-4

Itzig Josef was barely nineteen when Maurycy was born, but then if Sussel's tombstone is correct, she was seventeen.

Selig's Itzig Josef was undoubtedly named for Isak Josef who had died earlier in 1862 at age seventy-eight. Isak Josef was called just Josef without the Isak, as were all his namesakes, including my own grandfather's brother. So why should Selig's son be any different?

And Dawid Eisig's sister Anna could easily have been named for Selig's late wife Chana. It was all falling into place perfectly. I even began to consider that the reason my father had heard of Uncle Selig was somehow connected to his advanced age. Perhaps he reached a hundred, and it talked about. Perhaps he died when my father was old enough to have remembered.

Had Gittel and Salomon asked her grandfather Selig to be the sandak for their son? Very likely. Selig was neither sandak nor witness for the naming of Gittel or her brother Markus. But he could have been for Josef's older children, Maurycy and Freida. I do not have their birth records so cannot say.

So how do I prove that this Josef is Itzig Josef, the son of Selig? David's DNA had not shown significant, meaningful matches; and in any case, who did I want him to match?

I realized that since David had tested, another dozen Pikholz descendants had joined the project so I reexamined David's results. I asked David's half-sister Anna to test, and she did. Anna has no endogamy issues on her mother's side either. I asked Zygmundt's son to test, and he declined.

DNA results

The question of whom to check for matches had only one answer. If I want to test to determine if Josef is Selig's son, I need to compare Josef's descendants to Selig's descendants. But we have no known descendants of Selig.

What we do have are fifteen descendants (at the time of this writing) of Selig's putative sister, my great-great-grandmother, Rivka Feige. But that means we are testing two hypotheses at once—that Josef is Selig's son and that Selig is Rivka Feige's brother. This is like trying to cross a divided street with two traffic lights on the basis of the far light being green. If the close light is red, you are liable to get run over. By reality.

In theory, even with good genetic matches Josef could be related to Rivka Feige (or even her Pikholz husband Isak Fischel!) without this having anything to do with Selig. Perhaps she had another brother we don't know about. Or perhaps Josef's unknown father was a brother or nephew of Isak Fischel.

Nonetheless, with everything else fitting so nicely, I think that it is reasonable to make that leap. I can do that if David and Anna match my personal family, in which case they would be our fourth cousins. Depending on DNA for fourth cousins can be an iffy thing, but let us look at the numbers.

| | Suggested relationships | | Actual |
	Anna	David	relationships
Aunt Betty	3-5 cousin	2-4 cousin	3C1R
Uncle Bob	3-5 cousin	3-5 cousin	3C1R
Cousin Herb	3-5 cousin	3-5 cousin	3C1R
Israel	no match	no match	4th cousin
Sarajoy	no match	5-remote	4th cousin
Amy	4-remote	3-5 cousin	4th cousin
Jean	4-remote	4-remote	4th cousin
Judith	3-5 cousin	no match	4th cousin
Lee	4-remote	2-4 cousin	4th cousin
Rhoda	5-remote	no match	4th cousin
Terry	5-remote	no match	4th cousin
Marty	4-remote	4-remote	4th cousin
Joe	no match	no match	4th cousin
Elaine	5-remote	4-remote	4th cousin
Ralph	no match	no match	4C1R

Figure 7-5

First the level of matches as provided by FTDNA. 3C1R is third cousin once removed, etc. The first three, who are my father's generation, are reasonable for both Anna and David. The others are not as good, especially Anna's matches.

The results are much more interesting when we look at the chromosomes.

The numbers that follow are from GEDmatch, and I have looked only at those chromosomes where at least one match is greater than 10 cM. There is some debate about using smaller segments, and I am generally on the side of those who will use the smaller matching segments (See Chapter Ten.) In this case, I have chosen to be conservative, perhaps to make up for challenging the double traffic light.

I have only included segments where more than one person matches Anna or David.

Chromosome	Match	Anna			David		
		Start Location	End Location	cM	Start Location	End Location	cM
3	Amy	45,789,098	128,946,298	67.9	106,024,927	129,372,065	22.2
	Herb	45,698,438	128,428,440	67.4	106,024,927	128,428,440	21.2
	Jean	45,789,098	118,285,250	57.9	106,024,927	118,271,041	11.7
	Judith	45,789,098	73,985,797	33.7			
	Lee	74,412,529	127,165,020	31.3	128,551,350	138,548,552	9.8
	Uncle Bob	44,859,651	81,294,204	39.9			
	Aunt Betty	44,859,651	123,611,447	62.0	105,353,636	123,779,337	15.8
8	Herb	52,493,571	71,508,725	18.6	49,760,720	71,524,644	20.0
	Aunt Betty	52,493,571	71,292,924	18.4	52,662,702	71,524,644	18.7
	Uncle Bob	52,662,702	71,292,924	18.2	52,662,702	71,524,644	18.7
15	Marty	73,252,521	99,236,481	50.0	73,270,805	93,980,394	34.7
	Herb	91,608,779	98,928,088	22.6			
	Rhoda	93,282,630	95,272,025	6.7			
21	Rhoda	9,849,404	19,857,832	16.4			
	Terry	9,849,404	19,644,504	16.1			
	Lee	15,882,461	19,769,937	9.2			

Figure 7-6

Anna matches my family on four different chromosomes; David on only two. On chromosome 15, Anna matches Marty over 50 cM and Herb over 22.6 cM, with a smaller match with Rhoda in the same segment. On chromosome

21, Anna matches Rhoda and Terry on a segment of just over 16 cM, with a smaller match with Lee in the same place.

On chromosome 8, both David and Anna match Aunt Betty, Uncle Bob, and Herb over 18-20 cM in the same place. Note the congruent locations of some of those matches.

Chromosome 3 is where Anna has really excellent matches of over 62 cM with Herb, Aunt Betty, and my sister Amy; and 57.9 cM with my sister Jean. Uncle Bob and my sister Judith have between 30 and 40 cM starting where the others start, and Lee has 31.3 cM starting in the middle of the others and carrying on to near the end. David matches five of the seven with much smaller but still respectable segments.

In my opinion, the matches on chromosome 3 alone are enough to demonstrate with a high degree of certainty that Anna and David are our fourth cousins.

Note: Joe, Elaine, and Ralph, the descendants of my great-grandfather's two sisters, do not match either Anna or David in any significant way, therefore they do not appear in Figure 7-6.

Siblings

Since Anna and David have all their Jewish DNA from their father, the fact that they have different mothers is not relevant for this study. Despite the fact that they are brother and sister, there is a large difference between their matches with my personal family, both on chromosomes 15 and 21 and on chromosome 3. In all those cases, Anna's matches are much stronger than David's.

On chromosome 8, Aunt Betty and Uncle Bob have nearly identical matches with both Anna and David. My sisters and I do not have these matches, even in small segments. This may mean that my father did not have the segment that his brother and sister have, and it may mean that he did but did not pass it along to the five of us.

On chromosome 3, my sister Amy has a very large match (67.9 cM) with Anna. Jean shares most of that segment and Judith about half of it. Neither my sister Sarajoy nor I received this segment at all.

There is a message here. The more people who test, the better results you are likely to get. Not every time, but enough of the time to make it worthwhile.

You cannot say "My sister tested. Why do I need to test too?" Her results will be different. Often significantly so.

You certainly cannot say "My second cousin tested so my family is already represented. Why do you need me?" Every branch of a family has significant amounts of DNA that other branches do not.

My second cousin Lee has a nice match that he shares with my sisters on chromosome 3, but the other second cousins do not. Lee, Rhoda, and Terry match Anna on chromosome 21, but we do not and neither does Marty. Marty has large segments that match both Anna and David on chromosome 15, but aside from a small match between Rhoda and Anna, the other second cousins do not match here at all.

Can we cross this street?

The one question that remains is this. We have a green light that shows the relationship between Josef's great-grandchildren Anna and David on one hand and Rivka Feige's descendant on the other. But is that enough to allow us to put Selig in between? Can we ignore the red light and cross the street based on the green light alone? That is a decision that each genetic genealogist must answer based on his own judgment.

Figure 7-7

62

My own judgment guides me to these conclusions:

a)   Josef Pikholz, the ancestor of Anna and David, is in fact Itzig Josef (b. 1862) the son of Selig Pikholz.

b)   Selig is indeed my great-grandfather's uncle as my father had said. He is the brother of my great-great-grandmother Rivka Feige, not her husband Isak Fischel, and is almost certainly the son of Isak Josef (~1784-1862).

c)   On my website and in my database, I am leaving Rivka Feige and Selig as siblings but without naming the parents, despite the fact that I am quite sure that their father is Isak Josef. I would like to find one more piece of evidence, and towards that end, we are trying to find a death record for Uncle Selig.

d)   I am not prepared to draw conclusions about the identity of the mother of Rivka Feige and Selig.

Chapter Eight

Nachman, Gabriel, and Moshe

The connection of the family of David and Anna's great-grandfather Josef to my personal family using DNA and bypassing the two unproven connections with Uncle Selig is not our only instance of crossing a divided street based on the green light on the far side. We have a similar street separating Nachman and Moshe where I think, but cannot yet prove, that Gabriel is the generation in between.

Moshe

Moshe Pikholz lived in Skalat in the latter half of the 1800s. He was married to Chana, the daughter of Tobias and Matel Muhlrad, and they had ten children—the first born in 1874 and the last in 1894. There were two married daughters whose families were murdered in the Holocaust, a third married daughter who may have had two grandsons who survived the Holocaust, and a daughter Cirel about whom we know nothing beyond her 1894 birth.

Two of their six sons, Nachman and Gabriel, died before their second birthdays. A son Chaim was killed in the Holocaust as were his five children. A son Zalman is said to have died in the 1930s with no children. A son Getzel had two children who survived the Holocaust, but neither of them had children. One son Tobias, born 1882, was killed in the Holocaust but three of his daughters survived—one coming to Israel in the 1930s, the other two after the war. These three daughters have a total of six children living in Israel, Australia, and the United States.

Much of the information I have about this family came from Getzel's daughter Miriam, born Matel, who died in 2002 at age eighty-eight. Miriam did not know her grandfather Moshe, nor did she know his father's name, but she thought he had died young, perhaps in his forties.

Moshe and Nachman

I have discussed Nachman in Chapter One where I showed that his Y male-line DNA matches my own and in Chapter Five where I demonstrated that he is the father of Rita's great-great-grandfather Moshe Hersch. We have a death record for Nachman in May 1865 at age seventy, which tells us he was born about 1795.

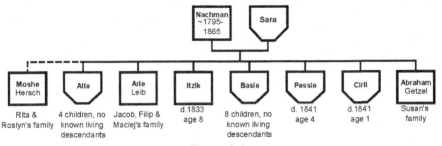

Figure 8-1

The relatively uncommon names Nachman and Getzel appear in both Nachman's family and Moshe's, so it is natural to suspect a connection between them.

Moshe's first son Nachman was born in January 1879, pointing to the likelihood that he was named for the Nachman who had died thirteen and a half years earlier. Since Moshe had his children over twenty years beginning in 1874, I considered it unlikely that Nachman (born 1795) was his father, but he could easily have been Moshe's grandfather.

Gabriel and Moshe

In the way of the world, some of the Pikholz families from Skalat lived in other towns in the area, and often those are easily identified in the records, particularly when the Pikholz is the woman. Galician birth records after 1876 name the mothers' parents, but not the fathers'.

One particular group of records refer to a couple named Gabriel and Sara Pikholz who lived in Husiatyn, about 27 miles SSE of Skalat. The first source was Jewish Records Indexing-Poland (JRI-Poland). There is an index reference for a death record from 1844 for Schaje, age four, with no mention of his parents. JRI-Poland also has the 1851 birth of Moses to Gabriel and Sara. Both of these records are in the AGAD archives in Warsaw.

JRI-Poland also shows a birth record from Podwoloczysk in 1893 for a daughter Brane born to Joel and Chancie Halpern. Chancie is identified as the daughter of Gabriel and Sara Pikholz from Husiatyn. Later this family was filled out with three more Halpern children from records in the All Galicia Database and the Czernowitz BMD Index Database.

We have a set of 1816-1876 death records from the Lwow archives via the Family History Center in Salt Lake City. That set includes the 1852 death of Gabriel, age 30, in which he is identified as being "aus Skalat," from Skalat. It is not clear if that means he lived in Skalat but died in Husiatyn or that he lived in Husiatyn but had come from Skalat.

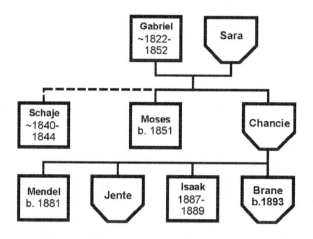

Figure 8-2

It is easy to surmise that Gabriel and Sara's son Moses born in 1851 is the same Moshe who appears to be the grandson of Nachman. That Moshe named his third son Gabriel, a rare name indeed among the Pikholz descendants. The scenario that suggests itself is that Moshe named his first son Nachman after his own grandfather whom he knew, his second son Tobias after his wife's father, and his third son Gabriel after the father he never knew. Gabriel's Moses was born in 1851, which fits well with Moshe's children who were born between 1874 and 1894.

There is one death record for an adult Moshe Pikholz in Skalat between the birth of Moshe's youngest daughter Cirel in 1894 and the birth of the granddaughter Miriam in 1913. That is in 1894, which fits Miriam's recollection that Moshe had died in his forties. We cannot be sure, however, because that 1894 death record says that Moshe was fifty-seven, not forty-three. That may be an error, but it cannot be dismissed out of hand.

Nachman and Gabriel

Gabriel who died at age thirty in 1852 would fit right in as a son—possibly the eldest—of Nachman. Aside from the age on the 1894 death record, the logic is impeccable.

It is not, however, good enough for a responsible genealogist. My own rule as I have presented it in my lecture *Beyond A Reasonable Doubt*[1] is that in the absence of unambiguous documentation, once you reach the point that you know something to be correct, do not record it until you find one more piece of supporting evidence.

In this case, DNA comes to mind.

Here there are two crossings to be made in order to reach the other side. It must be demonstrated that Gabriel is Nachman's son, and it must further be demonstrated that Moshe in Skalat is the same Moses who was born to Gabriel in Husiatyn.

It is possible in theory that the Pikholz is not Gabriel, but his wife Sara; however, she cannot be the daughter of Nachman because Nachman's wife is known to be Sara, and she would not have had a daughter with the same name.

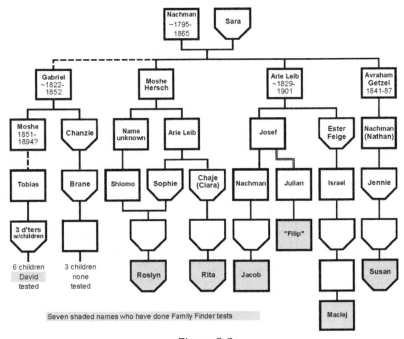

Figure 8-3

Y-DNA is not relevant here because Moshe has no male-line descendants, nor do we know of any for Gabriel.

As it happens, Brane, the daughter of Chancie Halpern and granddaughter of Gabriel and Sara, has three living grandchildren in the Jerusalem area. None of them is willing to have anything to do with the Pikholz Project, let alone do a genetic test. Their father was born in cosmopolitan Vienna, and they do not care to acknowledge that their grandmother came from a small town in east Galicia. What the grandson actually said in Hebrew was "We aren't from Galicia; WE are from VIENNA." And I could hear his nose in the air over the phone.

Without the cooperation of the descendants of Gabriel, crossing the divided street from Moshe to Nachman can only be done by comparing the test results of the six descendants of Nachman with the DNA of some of the descendants of Moshe. Since the beginning of our DNA project, I tried to convince one of them to test and finally during the December 2014 sale at FTDNA, David, the son of Moshe's granddaughter Cyla, agreed. I would have liked one or two more of this family to test, but as usual, I take what I can get.

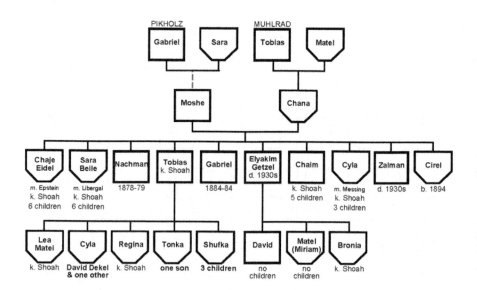

Figure 8-4

David Dekel

The descendants of Moshe Pikholz and his wife Chanzie Muhlrad are outlined in Figure 8-4. I summarized the fate of this family earlier in this chapter. There are six living great-grandchildren, children of the three surviving daughters of Tobias and his wife Feige Bomse.

I compared David Dekel on a GEDmatch chromosome browser to five known descendants of Nachman. The sixth, Rita, is not considered a match to David at all—neither by FTDNA nor by GEDmatch. That is not unreasonable for a fourth cousin once removed. I looked at the matches of ten cM or more, not wanting to jump to conclusions based on smaller segments.

CHROMOSOME 1:
- David has a match with Filip of 29 cM that includes a matching segment of 10.8 cM with Maciej.
- David has additional matches with Maciej of 10.2 cM and 15.5 cM on the same chromosome.

CHROMOSOME 7:
- David has a match of 22.6 cM with Susan.
- He also has nearly congruent segments of 12.5 and 12.7 cM with Filip and Jacob and another of 14.4 cM with Maciej.

CHROMOSOME 10:
- David has a segment of 10.8 cM in common with Rita's cousin Roslyn.

CHROMOSOME 11:
- David has a match of 12.5 cM with Maciej.

CHROMOSOME 20:
- David has overlapping matches of 25.5 and 11.3 cM with Filip and Maciej.

All these matches together appear to demonstrate that David's great-grandfather Moshe is a descendant of Nachman. It does not demonstrate that the link between them is Gabriel. I would like to see a couple of additional tests in David's family and, of course, some from Gabriel's family. I would expect that Gabriel's descendants' matches with both sides of the traffic light will be stronger than they are with each other.

David and the other Skalaters

Just as the other descendants of Nachman have matches with other Pikholz descendants, so does David. Most of those are not particularly large nor do they seem to fit a pattern—they are likely from the Pikholz family in the more distant past.

But something is different with David. David has much better matches with the other Skalat Pikholz descendants than Nachman's other descendants. He has forty-three matches of over 10 cM with other Pikholz descendants, including one of 26.4 cM. It appears that David has a Pikholz connection—at least one—which is not from Nachman.

Of particular interest are two segments on chromosome 23, one of 12.2 cM and one of 9.3 cM. This is the X chromosome, which men get only from their mothers. In both cases, David's X-matches are with women. This cannot be a match from Nachman because it would have to have gone through Moshe and Tobias, which is impossible.

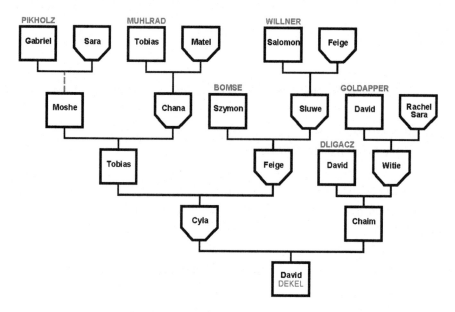

Figure 8-5

70

It appears, therefore that this Pikholz DNA came from David's Bomse grandmother or his Muhlrad or Willner great-grandmothers. Or possibly Gabriel's wife. Unfortunately, we do not have the diversity of cousins in David's family that we would need for further analysis. Except from Gabriel's descendants.

Chapter Nine

Too Good to be True?

The Rosenblooms

Not all of my genetic genealogy work has been about the Pikholz families where dozens of known descendants have tested. Sometimes the results of a single, unsolicited test just fit right in to complete a story. Or so it appears.

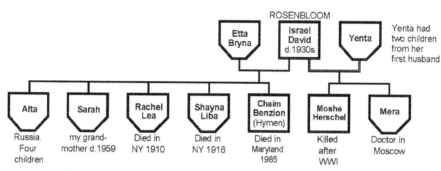

Figure 9-1

My maternal grandmother, Sarah Rosenbloom Gordon, died when I was eleven without our ever having had much conversation. For that matter, she never told my mother much about her family or her life in Europe. Later when I wanted to know about the past, I went to her younger brother, Uncle Hymen.

Uncle Hymen—Chaim Benzion—was born in 1894, and his mother died shortly before his second birthday. His father, my great-grandfather and namesake Israel David Rosenbloom, remarried soon after and the household soon expanded to include two children from the second marriage as well as two that the second wife had brought with her.

Uncle Hymen left Russia for the United States at age twenty, knowing little about his mother's family. He did not know her parents' names or if she had brothers and sisters. He didn't know his mother's maiden name. She probably died in her late thirties, so she could well have had living parents; he didn't remember.

Her family could have lived in another town, perhaps a few hours away. Perhaps they lived in Borisov and he knew them, but didn't know them to be family. Perhaps there were questions I could have asked which would have triggered memories, but I didn't know enough to ask them.

The family in the United States knew little of the eldest sister Alta Kaplan. She had four children, and Uncle Hymen knew the names of three. Two of her sons were married, and each had a daughter. But when Stalin closed the borders, all contact ceased. Somehow, my grandmother learned that her father, Israel David, died sometime in the 1930s.

Alta Rosenbloom Kaplan, with son Yaakov (seated), daughter Etta Bryna, and two sons, one of whom is Baruch Yosef. Sometime in the 1920s.

Figure 9-2

Mera

Uncle Hymen was particularly close to the two younger children from his father's second marriage—even more so after his three older sisters left for New York. He named his first son after his half-brother, Moshe Herschel, who had been killed in the aftermath of the First World War.

After WWI the family moved, or was moved, from Borisov in today's Belarus to Penza in interior Russia. The little sister Mera grew up to become a physician and lived in Moscow. In 1929, she asked Uncle Hymen to send her one of those new-fangled instruments with tubes you put in your ears so you can hear a patient breathe. She included her mailing address along with her name "M. D. Goldina." In Russian, Goldina is the feminine form of Goldin. It is the only record we have of her married name. The "D" would have been Davidovna, her patronymic, based on her father's second name. Her husband's given name was a mystery.

Uncle Hymen (right) with Moshe Herschel, Mera, and older sister Shayna Liba

Figure 9-3

Uncle Hymen said to me more than once that she may well be alive, but that was in the 1970s when finding people in Russia was not considered realistic.

In April 2014, a Facebook friend in California, Luba Tabolova, told me that the Malakhovskoye Cemetery in Moscow is online with photographs, and that she had found the grave of Mera Davidovna Goldin, born 1903, died 1990. With her in the same grave is Maks Yankelovitch Goldin born 1905, died 1979. Further inquiry told us that she was from Penza. Normally the records would have an occupation, but in this case, she was simply "retired."

There was little question that this was my grandmother's half-sister and her husband.

Luba looked further for evidence of a Goldin with the patronymic Maksovitch, but nothing panned out as a possible first cousin to my mother. I would like to have found a living descendant of Aunt Mera. Such a cousin might even know something about the family of the eldest sister, Alta Kaplan.

David

Days after Luba's discovery of Aunt Mera's grave, I was doing a routine check of my new Family Finder matches and I saw the following.

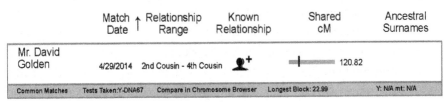

Match Date ↑	Relationship Range	Known Relationship	Shared cM	Ancestral Surnames

Mr. David Golden	4/29/2014	2nd Cousin - 4th Cousin		120.82	
Common Matches	Tests Taken:Y-DNA67	Compare in Chromosome Browser	Longest Block: 22.99	Y: N/A mt: N/A

Figure 9-4

David Goldin, a suggested second-fourth cousin. If Aunt Mera had a son, he would be my half-first cousin once removed, so that's close enough. And she very well may have named him after her father. So chalk up another victory for DNA matching.

If only my mother were here. And Uncle Hymen's daughter who had died only months before. I wrote her a letter on my blog telling her what I had discovered with Luba's help. I was excited beyond words.

David Goldin's profile on FTDNA had an email address, and I wrote to him.

> *Dear Sir,*
> *I see that we have a close DNA match - second-fourth cousin.*
>
> *My grandmother had a half-sister named Mera Goldin who was a physician in Moscow. Our last contact with her was in 1929.*
>
> *Is it possible after all these years that this is your family? If so, please tell me where you are and how and when I can reach you by phone.*
>
> *Israel David Pickholtz*
> *Jerusalem*

A day later, I received a note from a man in Massachusetts, a nephew of David Goldin. David had tested at the nephew's request but asked that he not have to deal with inquiries such as mine. The nephew didn't say how old David is, but David's father (1910-1983) was born in Suffolk County, New York, and he had lived his whole life there. David's grandfather went to the U.S. from Poland. So David is clearly neither son nor grandson of Aunt Mera.

Sometimes the old phrase "too good to be true" is just that.

The nephew gave me the maiden names of David's mother and grandmothers, and they don't mean anything to me in the context of my family.

I was nonetheless curious about the very close connection. It was not uniquely close, as I had dozens of matches in the third cousin range whose actual connection to my family is unknown. But after I thought I had found a living first cousin of my mother, I didn't want to just discard him like a piece of scrap paper.

At the time, I was the only one of our Rosenbloom descendants to have tested. During the months that followed, my four sisters, two first cousins and two second cousins joined me. David himself, through his nephew since he does not want anyone bothering him, was gracious enough to give me access to his kit so I could do a thorough evaluation of the possible connection between us. Just for the challenge.

In fact, that connection has nothing to do with my Rosenbloom side. But just for fun, I'll tell you that his Y-37 matches the Y-37 of a test on my mother's father's (Gordon) side, though not perfectly.

Etta Bryna

Although I would really like to learn more about the families of my grandmother's sisters Alta Kaplan and Mera Goldin, perhaps even finding a living descendant, my main challenge with the Rosenblooms is working backwards in time. I know the names of my great-grandfather's parents, Yaakov and Shayna Liba, but nothing else. No siblings, for instance. There were two other Rosenblooms in Borisov, but we have nothing that connects the three families.

My second cousin Sam did a Y-37 test on the Rosenbloom line and came up with a total of only three matches—two, three and four mutations away. None of the three has done a Family Finder test, so that for now is a dead end.

The bigger challenge is my great-grandmother. As I wrote above, we know almost nothing about her. We have a photo of her grave, and from that, we know that her father was Yehudah and that he was a Levi.[1] Her children were born from about 1880 until 1894, though we know she had additional sons who died. Because of those sons, Uncle Hymen was given the name Chaim (=life) for good luck. I figure she was probably born in the late 1850s and was in her late thirties when she died in 1896.

We do know one other very important thing about Etta Bryna. We know what her mitochondrial DNA looked like. It's the same as my own in haplogroup U1b1. When I had my MtDNA tested in 2011, there were six perfect matches. But that information itself does not mean much. According to the Beginner's Guide at the FTDNA Learning Center, a perfect MtDNA match means a common ancestor within five generations with 50 percent confidence and within 22 generations with 95 percent confidence. In other words, these perfect matches could mean nothing more than a common ancestor two or three hundred years ago or more. That isn't very useful.

When I looked at the Family Finder results for those who took that test, none of those perfect matches appeared to be useful. One was a suggested "fourth-remote cousin" and another a "fifth-remote cousin" but that was it. I saw no point in looking that far back for a family about whom I knew so little.

I checked back with this list of matches from time to time. A seventh perfect match was with Ralph Henry Baer. I learned from his 2014 obituaries that his "Brown Box" invention eventually went on sale as the first video game "Odyssey." But he was not a Family Finder match.

The tenth match was different. In September 2013, I saw a perfect match with Deborah Sirotkin Butler, but this time we had a Family Finder match as suggested "third-fifth cousins." We discussed our families online and we subsequently found ourselves sitting together at a lecture in Salt Lake City in 2014, but we saw nothing we could work with.

In 2014, there were two more perfect matches, both matching on Family Finder, but here too they were suggested "fourth-remote" and "fifth-remote" cousins.

One more match showed up in early 2015, but with something very encouraging. Bernard is a perfect MtDNA match and a suggested "third-fifth cousin" on Family Finder, like Deborah Butler, but he listed his most distant ancestor as Yenta Bryna Knott. His is Yenta Bryna, mine is Etta Bryna. This looked good.

The kit is managed by Bernard's cousin Leonid. Yenta Bryna Knott is their great-grandmother, born in Lodz about ten years after my great-grandmother. These two women could easily have been first or second cousins, named for the same person. There is the little matter of 412 miles (664 km) between Lodz and Borisov, but even then, cousins could have lived far apart.

Leonid sent me a small photograph of his great-grandmother (Figure 9-5), which is one more than I have of my own.

Figure 9-5

He also showed me her New York death certificate with the name Yetta rather than Yenta. It lists her parents as Shmul Mendel and her mother as Sarah Rywka Knot. Leonid says that's an error and that the family knows that Knott was Yenta Bryna's father's name.

Unfortunately, that is as far as we go, for now.

DNA research is a long game. You cannot expect to walk in and find meaningful matches right away. When you do, chances are the person you match has been waiting patiently (or impatiently) for a few years. We do our tests and make them available, not so much to find people, but to enable people who come along later to find *us*.

Sam has only three Y-37 matches, but a few tomorrows from now, or a few years of tomorrows, may bring him a match for an actual close relative. And we certainly seem to be a little closer to Etta Bryna than we were before our latest match.

Nor does DNA provide the whole solution. It supports our traditional research methods and sometimes gives us new directions. There is always more work to do. If it were really that simple, it would indeed be too good to be true.

---

[1] The male-line descendants of the Biblical Levi served in the Temple in Jerusalem, in a supportive role to the Kohanim, the priests. People maintain this tradition even today. Tombstones of Leviim often have carvings of pitchers signifying their role in washing the hands of the Kohanim. They were also the singers in the Temple.

Chapter Ten

Small Segments: Gold or Fool's Gold?

All Those Genetic Cousins

The most elementary premise in genetic genealogy is "You get your DNA from your parents," followed by "You pass your DNA to your children." Those statements are at once basic and obvious. Those strings of As and Ts and Gs and Cs that comprise our DNA come half from our fathers and half from our mothers. Within our cells, our mothers' DNA and our fathers' DNA are maintained separately. Before they passed them on to us, they recombined what they received from their own parents, just as we do before passing DNA to our children.

The results we receive from the testing companies are not a list of those four letters, each appearing thousands upon thousands of times, although that raw data is available to us. The results we receive from the testing companies are lists of people we match, people whose patterns of G and C and A and T match ours in specific places. Those matching segments are available to us on chromosome browsers like the one in Figure 10-1, either from the testing companies or from third-party tools such as GEDmatch, based on the raw data.

There can be thousands of such matches, and as more people join the world of genetic genealogy, those numbers will increase substantially. When I first did my Family Finder test, I had a little over 2000 matches, a number that has more than doubled in two years. We want to find our relatives inside that haystack of "relatives."

Illustrative. Not necessarily to scale.
Figure 10-1

The matches on the chromosome represented in Figure 10-1 above show my matches greater than one cM with one of my sisters (at the top), followed by a first, second, third and fourth cousin. As most of us would find intuitive, with each passing generation, the matching segments are fewer and for the most part smaller. Large segments can remain intact for several generations, but in general, our intuition is valid.

This seems to be pretty straightforward. Our quest is to find other people who have segments that match ours—the more and the larger, the better. Those matching segments came from what must be a common ancestor and having determined that, we then want to find that ancestor.

Identical Segments

When I first entered the world of genetic testing, I began following the blogs and learned that the experienced hands divided matching segments into two categories: Identical by Descent (IBD) and Identical by State (IBS). The former were considered highly reliable and the latter not so much. In general, the distinction was by the size of the segment. There was some debate about where to draw the line between the two and how exactly to judge reliability. I did not find all the talk convincing, and I found that some of the logic sounded circular. I was certainly not convinced by declarations (or impressive-looking charts) that segments of X cM were statistically Y percent likely to be IBD, and I did not consider these to be plans for action.

More than anything, I did not understand where people thought these IBS segments were coming from if not from our parents, i.e. by descent. I figured that if my sisters—even some of them—and I shared a small, congruent (or nearly so) segment, say 3 cM, then it was clear that we received it from our parents. And if we shared that same segment with Aunt Betty and Uncle Bob, then we obviously got it from our father and he got it from his parents. How could this be dismissed out of hand?

So they are small segments. Obviously, it seemed to me, segments did not remain 40+ cM indefinitely. Eventually they broke down through recombination and became smaller. And smaller still, eventually leaving us with some really small splinters. That's the way I saw it. "Splinters" seemed a better term than IBS anyway.

And how small is small? The default on the FTDNA chromosome browser is 5 cM, but it can be adjusted up to 10 cM or down to 3 cM or even 1 cM. The default at GEDmatch is 7 cM but that too can be adjusted, and in fact, I routinely raise it to 8 cM just to cut down on the number of matches. Individual experienced researchers draw their own lines.

I continued reading the blogs, the Facebook posts, and the wiki of the International Society of Genetic Genealogy (ISOGG). More than once, it was suggested that when extended and endogamous families lived in one place for a long time, IBS segments could come "from the population." [Thought I, "What, like a contagious disease, you get it from the water or the air?"] I read blogs and watched podcasted lectures about how to analyze autosomal matches. Some of these started with "First delete all your small matching segments."

The public discussion also examined the question by way of the name "Identical by State." Is this name accurate? Or meaningful? Perhaps "Identical by Chance" (IBC) would be a better name? Or maybe IBS and IBC should be separate categories—the former being real segments lost in the obscurity of the past and the latter a result of how the computer algorithm can combine alleles from both parents into one false segment.[1] Other labels were suggested.

What to do with matches on small segments

Correspondence with the experts was not getting me anywhere. I looked forward to face time with the teachers at the Genealogical Research Institute of Pittsburgh (GRIP) course "Practical Genetic Genealogy" in July 2014, where the instructors were some of the biggest names in the field. Blaine Bettinger explained that some of the small segments came about from bits that came from both parents and just looked like a single segment. That phenomenon is not confined to small segments.

Even two adjacent large segments can sometimes appear as one. Kitty Cooper writes:

> "[S]ometimes when you share two good sized segments (or one very large one which could be two next to each other), they come from two different ancestors, so the close cousin prediction is wrong."[2]

That sounded good to me, but I still figured that once they came together and stayed together they became useful as IBD from then on. In my example above, if my sisters and I share a small segment with Aunt Betty and Uncle Bob, it has become Identical by Descent from at least my grandparents, even if not from an earlier ancestor.

The most convincing argument came from CeCe Moore. She said that even if these small segments have a decent pedigree, they are probably from a common ancestor so far back that it is an inefficient use of time and energy to chase after them. That was language I could identify with!

When I met the following week in Salt Lake City with Kitty Cooper and Gaye Tannenbaum, the talk went to small segments. As I understood Kitty's approach, 10 cM or greater should be treated as IBD. Lesser segments might be. That made sense to me. In practical terms that meant that once I had a few people on a matching segment of 10 cM or more, I would accept potential family members with segments of 6-10 cM within the larger segment. Maybe even smaller ones.

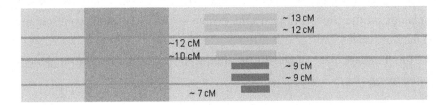

Figure 10-2 (illustrative)

I would normally take a pass on the small blue segments in Figure 10-2 but since they are included in the larger green ones, I treat them as probably significant.

Blogger Roberta Estes[3] has done a lot of work based on small segments, even without larger ones in the vicinity. Her arguments are convincing, but in my own endogamous families, I'd prefer to stay far away from the matching segments that are less than 5 or 6 cM. That is part of my decision to try to be responsibly conservative about my conclusions, and why I have adopted the policy of starting with segments larger than 10 cM and accepting smaller ones only when they fit in with the larger ones.

The British genetic genealogist Debbie Cruwys Kennett blogging at *Cruwys News* on 26 April 2015 ("Tracking DNA segments through time and space") finds what appears to be perfect triangulation with a potential cousin, until she runs into a surprising problem.

> *"[T]en of these [thirteen] segments are seemingly shared by me, my son and [paternal cousin] Mr K but are not shared with my father. Clearly this is a biological impossibility because if a segment is identical by descent (IBD) then by definition it must have been passed on from a parent to a child and it couldn't possibly skip a generation."*

Clearly, we must be very careful before drawing conclusions from small segments. CeCe Moore goes so far as to describe working with small segments as "folly."[4]

In the genetic genealogy community, the debate goes on, though some seem to consider it settled. Sometimes it can get acrimonious. The field is evolving, and new papers and blogs discuss both the science and the practical genealogy all the time. And positions evolve as the discussions continue and the data improves.

Jim Bartlett, part of the GEDmatch team, who has begun blogging at *segmentology.org*:

> *Date: Tue, Mar 17, 2015 at 6:30 PM*
> *From: Jim Bartlett*
> *Based on my experience so far, I think 7cM has a very high %*
> *IBD.*

> *Date: Mon, 20 Apr 2015 10:35:28 -0500 (CDT)*
> *From: Jim Bartlett*
> *The evidence is building that Triangulated segments, even*
> *in the range of 5-7cM (and maybe lower), are usually IBD.*

> *Date: Mon, 27 Apr 2015 15:55:05 -0400*
> *From: Jim Bartlett*
> *I dodged your question because, IMO, the centromere doesn't*
> *make any difference to me. I think Triangulation of*
> *segments over 5cM means they are IBD, virtually all of the*
> *time.*

The genealogist and blogger Michael Maglio writes of small segments in the 2.5 cM range.

> *"Why are these minimum segments important? My*
> *research shows that these segments stay in the gene pool*
> *for dozens of generations."[5]*

In that case, clearly they are useful, though probably less so for endogamous families.

Ann Turner addresses the question "How short is short?" and discusses the phenomena of fuzzy boundaries and compound segments.[6]

I could pile on additional sources, but by the time you see this dear reader, there will be more good quotes, positions will have changed and new ideas will have been proposed and debated.

For now, I have chosen an approach that serves my particular research, my particular family structure. Those are the important considerations. I shall work with matching segments of 10 cM or more and take into account those of 6-10 cM when they fit a larger segment, as in Figure 10-2. If I were working with a non-endogamous family, I would probably be more liberal. I would also have fewer matches to work with.

---

[1] Roberta Estes explains that is for instance one parent has a series of alleles that are all "A" and the other parent has a parallel series that are all "C," the child will match a stranger who has some combination of As and Cs. This she calls "Identical By Chance." (http://dna-explained.com/2015/05/14/parent-child-non-matching-autosomal-dna-segments/)

[2] http://blog.kittycooper.com/2015/03/using-your-dna-test-results-the-basics-for-genealogists/

[3] dnaexplained.com

[4] http://www.yourgeneticgenealogist.com/2014/12/the-folly-of-using-small-segments-as.html

[5] http://originsdna.blogspot.com/2015/03/breaking-through-autosomal-dna.html

[6] http://www.jogg.info/72/files/Turner.htm

Chapter Eleven

"I'm a Pikholz Too"

Organizing kits into "Projects"

Among the services that Family Tree DNA offers, is the possibility to open projects under their auspices. The purpose of these projects is to allow users to make their information available to one another in order to further collaborative research of different sorts, often scientific. The projects FTDNA offers on their "Join" page are Surname, Y-DNA Geographical, MtDNA Geographical, Dual geographical, MtDNA Lineage and Haplogroup Projects based on Y-DNA or MtDNA. There are a few others that are not presented on the "Join" page.

Participation in the project is free but opening a project requires FTDNA's approval, and they have a list of rules by which they expect the project administrators to abide. Some projects are open to anyone, and some require approval of prospective members by the project administrators.

I have joined projects for my R1b Y-DNA haplogroup and for my U1 MtDNA haplogroup. Frankly, I have no idea what the good folks running these projects are doing, but if my own DNA can be of help to them, I am fine with that.

I have, however, set up several surname projects for my own family members. These are not primarily for the research purposes that FTDNA intended, though it enables the kind of comparison I made in Chapter Four (Figure 4-4). I set them up simply to help me keep all my family kits in order and to allow myself access to every kit without having to log out and in every time I want to look at something.

I have surname projects called Pickholtz (for Pikholz descendants), Kwoczka, Rosenbloom, Gordon—Rachmiel (descendants of my third great-grandfather) and RosenzweigBauerZelinka (for my paternal grandmother's lines). Of course, I am a member of all five projects and every time I have a good, new match, I get notices from all of them.

In the summer of 2013, a man named Victor Weisskopf, whose name was totally unfamiliar to me, joined the Pickholtz project after seeing that he had matches with six [six!] of my kits, none of them close. In the months that followed with more Pikholz descendants tested, my blogs and Facebook posts attracted more attention, and other non-Pikholz began reporting large numbers of matches with the Pikholz descendants' kits. As the number of actual Pikholz kits grew, "large" was redefined from fifteen to twenty, twenty-five, and eventually "more than thirty." Many of those officially joined the project so that I'd be able to look at their matches efficiently. Some of them brought along the kits of their mothers, brothers and cousins, as well.

None of them brought Y-DNA matches that were at all close to our own, so we are not talking about male-line matches.

None of these people shared ancestral surnames with any of the Pikholz descendants and few shared much geography. I assumed that any common ancestors we shared were back in the mid-1700s when we had no surnames and there are no records with which to work. In one instance of false hope there was a match with a family named Waltman, and I had visions of two brothers in the lumber business, one became Pikholz (holz = wood) and the other Waltman (wald = forest). But we found that our matches were with the Waltman's spouse, so we had to cross that out.

It is necessary to keep in mind the most recent common ancestor of the known Pikholz descendants is probably not much earlier than 1770. These earlier matches would not match specifically with any of today's known families, but rather with the common Pikholz ancestor or at the level of his or her parents or grandparents.

In any case, I did quite a few FTDNA chromosome browsers on the kits of this group and a number of my weekly blog posts discussed the results.

More recently, as the number of Pikholz kits approached sixty, I took stock.

Figure 11-1 shows the matches as estimated by FTDNA of sixteen non-Pikholz at different levels, differentiated by Skalat, Rozdol and Others—that last category being Vladimir and Joyce. There were others who could have been in this analysis, but they did not join the surname project or did not upload their raw data to GEDmatch. So let us remember, this group is self-selected and does not purport to be a proper statistical sample.

After the first sixteen in this analysis is my second cousin Ruth who, despite being on my mother's side, shows a large number of Pikholz matches presumably via her father. Following Ruth is David Goldin from Chapter Nine.

The sixteen include three mother-child pairs. In all three instances, the child has more matches with the Pikholz descendants than does the mother; that means that the father also has Pikholz matches. But none of these fathers tested.

A few of the non-Pikholz have matches at the level of suggested second-fourth cousins and the third-fifth cousins may also be significant.

MATCHES OF SOME non-PIKHOLZ WITH PIKHOLZ DESCENDANTS, ON FTDNA

Name	Total	2-4 cousins				3-5 cousins			4-remote			5-remote			Totals		
		S	R	O	Who?	S	R	O	S	R	O	S	R	O	S	R	O
JoAnne	37	1			Dalia	1	2	1	11	4		14	3		27	9	1
Mark	37	1			Barbara	7	2		6	1	1	14	5		28	8	
JudiZ	31	1			Lloyd	2			7	4	1	14	2		24	6	1
SarahC	31	2			Dalia, Gene	4	1		5	1		15	3		26	5	0
Victor	35	1	1		Gili, Pawel	3			9	3	1	10	7		23	11	1
Cynthia	35					4	1	1	4	2		19	4		27	7	1
Alexandra	30		1		SteveP		1		4	1		17	5	1	21	8	1
David Ari	30	4			IP & sisters	3	2	1	9	3		8			24	5	1
Lily	30					7		1	7	1		11	3		25	4	1
Lily's mom	25					1	1	1	9	2		9	2		19	5	1
SteveT	37					6	2		10	3		11	5		27	10	0
Steve's mom	25			1	Vladimir	1			3	2		13	5		17	7	1
MarlaW	38					4	1		5	3		21	4		30	8	0
Marla's mom	33					3	1		3	3		17	6		23	10	0
SharonG	33	1			Elaine	9			8	2		8	5		26	7	0
GaryG	37					3	1		3	3	1	20	6		26	10	1
Ruth	34	8			My family	2	2		4	2		12	4		26	8	0
D. Goldin	33	3			Judith, Marty, IP	8	2		8	3		8	1		27	6	0

Ruth is a second cousin on my mother's side with many Pikholz matches.
I introduced David Goldin in Chapter Nine.

Figure 11-1

Matches with the Rozdol descendants

(See the known Rozdol relationships in Appendix D.)

JoAnne has a total of seven segments of more than 10 cM that match Rozdol descendants, the largest being 14.8 cM. There are no discernible patterns. Two Rozdolers are suggested third-fifth cousins; one of those two is included in the seven segments of more than 10 cM.

Mark has only five segments of 10 cM or more that match Rozdol descendants, the largest being 14.1 cM. He does, however, seem to show a pattern on the right end of chromosome 18. The four overlapping segments in Figure 11-2 shows Mark's matches with Micha, Pawel, Miriam, and Frances. You can ignore the 4.2 cM match with Micha, shown in pink.

Micha 63,984,412-70,229,546 - 12.924 cM	1
Pawel 66,197,579-69,983,715 - 8.22 cM	2
Miriam 66,197,579-69,717,063 - 7.235 cM	3
Francis 67,432,490-71,655,868 - 12.228 cM	4

Figure 11-2

Miriam's father and Francis' mother are second cousins of Micha, so the fact that Mark seems to match them as a group is significant. The common ancestral couple of this group are Pinchas Pikholz and Rachel Borek. Pawel's possible connection to this group will be discussed in Chapter Nineteen. Mark does not have these ancestral surnames, but one of the purposes of genetic research is to give our research new directions, not necessarily to deliver proof on a platter.

I went through the ritual of triangulation using the one-to-one tool on GEDmatch and was surprised to find that Micha does not match Miriam and Francis on this chromosome, nor do Miriam and Francis match each other. Normally when you match two people who do not match each other, it means that one of them is on your father's side and one on your mother's side. But here we have three people who do not match each other; Mark does not have three versions of chromosome eighteen. The only possibility is if some of these matches are IBS—not real matches—a subject I discussed in Chapter Ten.

Unless there is an error. So I tried the triangulation on FTDNA's chromosome browser.

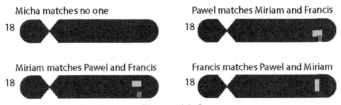

Figure 11-3

On FTDNA's chromosome browser, the triangulation makes more sense. Micha matches Mark on one side, and the other three match Mark on his other side. That can give Mark some direction in his research.

Judi has six matches in the 10-15 cM range, notable among them nearly congruent matches with Esther and Gary. They triangulate successfully. Their most recent common ancestral couple is Pikholz-Rosenzweig. None of Judi's matches is with people FTDNA suggests as third-fifth cousins or closer.

Sarah has six matching segments with the Rozdolers in the 10-15 cM range. Two of those are with Esther on the X chromosome. The other four are with the cousins Micha, Miriam and (twice) Francis. I haven't a clue if that might hint at something significant. Francis is the only match that FTDNA suggests as a third-fifth cousin.

Victor has seven matching segments of 10 cM or greater, none exceeding 14 cM. Two are with Pawel, who is a suggested second-fourth cousin and two others are with Esther.

Cynthia, Victor's second cousin, has five matching segments of 10 cM or more, the largest being nearly 14 cM. Two of the five are with Steve Peck and Esther on the X chromosome and another is with Francis. The significant match is with Pawel and Amos (who are first cousins once removed) on nearly congruent segments of about 11 cM. Neither Pawel nor Amos is suggested to be a close cousin, but Pawel is suggested as close to Victor, so there may well be something there. The ancestral surnames shared by Amos and Pawel are Pikholz, Mensch, Kranter and Klar, none of which are known in Cynthia and Victor's family. Nonetheless, there is some direction indicated here.

Alexandra has six matching segments of 10 cM or greater, the largest being 15.2 cM. Two of those are with Steve Peck, who FTDNA suggests as a second-third cousin. Another is with Esther who is a suggested third-fifth cousin. Nothing stands out with Esther's known cousins, but one of Steve's matches contains a segment that matches his second cousin Ira (9.4 cM). Their most recent common ancestral couple is Pikholz-Blum.

David Ari has five matching segments of over 10 cM, but one with Esther is 21.7 cM. He also has two segments over 10 cM with Francis and one with Miriam. The one with Miriam includes a 7 cM match with Francis. FTDNA suggests that David Ari is a third-fifth cousin to Miriam and Micha, so here too, the Pikholz-Borek couple may come into play.

In the three "mother-child" cases, I shall concentrate on the mothers so as not to confuse things with the fathers' matches. Lily's mother, Pamela—who is also a cousin of David Ari—has six matches of 10-16 cM with the Rozdolers. Three of those six are with Micha, who is a suggested third-fifth cousin according to FTDNA. Two others are with Rosa and Marion, who are double third cousins once removed. The match with Marion includes a segment of 7 cM with Rosa.

Steve Turner's mother has four matches greater than 10 cM, the largest being 13.8 cM. FTDNA suggests no one as close as third-fifth cousin.

Marla's mother has five matching segments over 10 cM, two of which are with Pawel. The largest—16.5 cM—is with Steve Peck who is a suggested third-fifth cousin. That segment includes a 5.6 cM segment with Steve's cousin Ira.

Sharon Goldstein has only three matches of over 10 cM—one with Pawel and two on the X chromosome with Esther. She has no suggested close matches among the Rozdolers.

My wife's third cousin Gary has seven matches greater than 10 cM. The largest (13.1 cM) is with Ira, who is a suggested third-fifth cousin. Two others are with Marion.

In the case of my second cousin Ruth, I am looking at possibilities involving her father's side. Ruth has two suggested third-fifth cousins among the Rozdolers—Steve Peck and Esther. She has eight segments of over 10 cM which match Rozdolers—three with Steve, two each with Esther and Gary, and one with Pawel on the X which must be from Pawel's mother's non-Pikholz side. On one match each with Steve and Esther, Ruth also matches our cousin Judy, but these do not triangulate. We can be certain that Ruth's connection on those two segments are on her father's side. I am pretty sure that few, if any, are not.

David Goldin has six matches of greater than 10 cM, none over 15 cM. Two of the six are with Amos and one with Gary—the two suggested third-fifth cousins.

So, of the whole group of non-Pikholz, there are only two—Mark and Victor/Cynthia—who seem to have a significant match with a particular part of the Rozdol family. Others have hints, and if it were my research, I might try to team up with others with similar hints to see if we matched each other. Of course, if we had thirty Rozdolers who had tested rather than the twelve we have, there might be better results.

Matches with the Skalat descendants

When it comes to matches between these non-Pikholz with the Pikholz descendants from Skalat, what I would expect is that the connection goes back to sometime in the mid- or early 1700s. That was before we had surnames, earlier than we have records, and earlier than the ancestor who begat the several Pikholz families in Skalat. In terms of DNA matches, that means I would expect to see matches not much greater than 10 cM with many of the Pikholz descendants with no particular pattern.

That is what we see for JoAnne, for instance. She has thirty-seven matching segments, six of which are on the X chromosome, with only one Pikholz match of interest. A match of nearly 16 cM with Dalia overlaps with matches with Susan and David Dekel. These matches triangulate. Dalia and Susan are from different families and David is probably a part of both.

JoAnne also has an X-chromosome of interest, matching Uncle Bob and four of my sisters on nearly congruent segments of 9-10 cM. Uncle Bob's X is from his mother, i.e. not a Pikholz, so these triangulating segments are from my paternal grandmother's side. Unfortunately, we don't have the cousins who can get more specific.

Mark is an actual Skalat descendant, so I would expect his matches to be better and more numerous. He has twenty-eight matches over 10 cM, but two of them (with Dalia and Barbara, in different places) are about 20 cM. His matches are consistent with common ancestors from the pre-surname period. Mark has near-congruent matches on the X chromosome (his mother's side) with Aunt Betty, Herb, and Terry. This was no surprise.

Judi has nineteen matching segments of 10-15 cM. It all appears to be pre-surname.

Sarah has twenty-five matching segments over 10 cM, including two of 26.6 and 21.5 cM. Six of the twenty-five matches are on Sarah's X chromosome.

Victor has fourteen matches of over 10 cM, several of them very interesting. It is noteworthy that only one of those matches is Gili, even though she is a suggested second-fourth cousin. Victor has matching segments with Barbara and Lloyd that triangulate. That points to the ancestral couple

Mordecai and Taube. On chromosome 18, Victor has matches of 10.7-12 cM with Ralph and Charles, together with smaller segments with Lee and Nan. These four are all descendants of Isak Josef. But also in this group of matches is a segment with Bruce Scharf, who is not known to be descended from Isak Josef. This points to a pre-surname match. Victor also has two significant matching segments with Roslyn, but not with other members of her family.

Cynthia has twenty matching segments of 10 cM or more with some remarkable diversity. Those include matches with six of the seven descendants of Nachman Pikholz. (only David Dekel is missing) highlighted by an X-chromosome match of 30.6 cM with Roslyn. She also has two matching segments with Gili—one of which also matches Rhoda, the other matches Elaine. This reinforces the "pre-surname" conclusion we see with Cynthia's cousin Victor. There may be a separate connection to the family of Nachman Pikholz.

Alexandra has sixteen matches over 10 cM, again spread across most of the Pikholz families. Her two largest matches are with Rita (16.3 cM) and Lee (17.3 cM). These two are nearly congruent and they triangulate. That match comes from an early pre-Pikholz ancestor from the pre-surname period.

David Ari has twenty-six matching segments of over 10 cM including a set of four of nearly 21 cM with three of my sisters and me. We cannot know if that is Pikholz or perhaps my grandmother's side or even my mother's. He has two other matches over 10 cM with several of my sisters and me, but we know that those are Pikholz since one includes Terry and the other includes Rhoda. David Ari's Pikholz matches are less diverse than most of the others, so it may come from a more recent source.

Lily's mother Pamela has twenty-eight matches over 10 cM plus one of 25 cM with Vladimir. Her matches, like those of her cousin David Ari, are not very diverse having almost nothing with the descendants of Nachman Pikholz. Some of her matches appear to be clearly with my grandmother's Hungarian/Slovakian side rather than with the Pikholz side. We have no matches that might determine which of my grandmother's sides.

Steve's mother Anna has five matches over 10 cM and two with Vladimir. One of those is over 20 cM. This does not give us much to go on.

Marla's mother has twenty matches over 10 cM, also without much to go on.

Sharon Goldstein joined our project because the European version of her paternal surname is the same as one of the sons-in-law of Nachman Pikholz. She has thirty-nine matches greater than 10 cM, eight of which are on the X chromosome. She has some interesting combinations including a match with two of my sisters and David Dekel. This one feels a bit better than some of the others, and I would be curious to see what matches we might find with some of her cousins.

Gary has ten matches of over 10 cM. Nothing stands out, though there is a match with both Craig and Bonnie. He has a match on the X with Craig that would be from their mothers' sides.

My cousin Ruth from my mother's side has thirty matches greater than 10 cM with some very interesting combinations. She has two places where she matches Aunt Betty and Uncle Bob together, one of which is 20 cM. She matches Aunt Betty and Marty, Aunt Betty and Pinchas of the Kwoczka cousins, Ron and me, Uncle Bob, Cousin Joe and me, Uncle Bob, Barbara, and Mr. X. There is also a tangle of matches on the X chromosome that appears to have some inconsistencies. She also has a match with her Jaffe cousin Judy and Jacob Laor, who has no known connection to the Jaffes. It would be interesting to find out more about Ruth's father's family and perhaps involve some of her family on his side.

David Goldin has thirty matching segments between 10 cM and 14 cM. Most of these are with parts of my own family including overlapping triangulated segments. I include in that definition Leonora, Dalia, and Barbara who are descendants of Mordecai and Taube. On two of those segments with multiple matching segments, David also has matches with Gili (with Barbara and Marty) and Gene (with Barbara and Leonora). Gili and Gene are descendants of Peretz Pikholz, so this points to another pre-surname match.

None of these pre-surname matches is a surprise. If your match with the Skalat Pikholz families is from after 1800, you should expect to find some matching surnames or at least matching geography. We do not know how far back the Pikholz families were in Skalat nor where they were before that. Therefore, if you have neither matching surnames nor matching geography, then it is fairly certain that your connection with the Pikholz families goes back to before Original Skalat Pikholz who was probably born around the 1750s. It may not matter if you have fifteen such matches or forty such matches. There is definitely a relationship, but it will have to be found using traditional genealogy tools—which don't go back far enough for our purposes.

Chapter Twelve

Sarah Baar and Breine Riss

For reasons I will not go into here, I am neither a fan of nor a participant in large, commercial online family trees. I am, however, a subscriber to Ancestry, which I use to search for documents, so from time to time I search my names of interest among their *"Public Member Trees."* Usually any Pikholz who turns up in such a search is someone I already know on a tree submitted by someone on the non-Pikholz, other side of the family. Occasionally there will be a previously unknown individual or small family, but never a completely new multigenerational family.

In November 2014, an unfamiliar name showed up. Sarah Pickholz was married to Eisig Baar and there was a list of four daughters, eight sons, and assorted grandchildren. The dates included Eisig's death in 1900 and the birth of one of the sons in 1874. The names of some of the children—Berti, Rudolph and Gustav—gave the impression that they lived in central Europe, not eastern Galicia.

I wrote to the tree owner, Milton Baar in Australia, and the opening volley went like this:

IsraelP

I see you have references to Sarah Pickholz on your Baar Ancestry.com tree.

We have many Sarah but I am not clear on who this is.

I am doing single-surname research on the Pikholz families and would be interested to hear who you are, how you are connected and what else you might happen to know.

I would prefer email contact: IsraelP@pikholz.org I also blog at http://allmyforeparents.blogspot.com

Milton

Sarah Pickholz is my great grandmother on my father's side. Not sure what additional information I can provide...?

Milton knew that the family had lived in Hranice and Freiburg in Czechoslovakia. Hranice is known as Mährisch Weisskirchen in German. Eastern Galicia meant nothing to Milton. But for a Pikholz woman having children in the 1870s, east Galicia is probably where to look—not only for her, but for at least some of her children—so I turned to JRI-Poland and searched "Surname sounds like Baar" and "Given Name sounds like Eisig."

There are three listings for births to Eisig and Sura Baar in Jagielnica, a town with several Baar families about 35 miles from Skalat. The children born there are Rifka (1865), Roisa (1867), and Juda (1869). Milton's Regina, Rosa, and Julius looked like good candidates. Jagnielnica birth records are available from 1860, so it appeared that these three were the eldest and perhaps the rest of the children were born in what became Czechoslovakia.

I wanted to learn what I could about the descendants of Sarah and Eisig, but perhaps more important, I wanted to identify Sarah's parents. Surely, they were from Skalat and were related to some other family that we already know. I know a handful of pre-1860 Sara Pikholz in Skalat, but they are all accounted for—either too old or married to other people.

Milton knew of two children each for Anna, David, Emil (his own grandfather), Josef, Regina, and Gustav; three each for Julius, Rosa, and Victor (Victor's without names); four for Moritz; none for Berti; and no information for Rudolph. Milton actually knows all three of Josef's grandchildren.

Gustav and Berti had lived in the United States. Many of the others were known or presumed to have been killed in the Holocaust. Much of the Baar family did not self-identify as Jews and had intermarried, but that did not save them. There are a few others on Milton's tree who may be alive.

I went to work putting together what I could and immediately found a grandson of Gustav on the *JewishGen Family Finder*, a site where people can list the families they are interested in. I also found that the 1900 death for Eisig was someone else, not Sarah's husband. Sarah's Eisig died in Hranice in 1908. There was no trace of a death record for Sarah, a record that might show her parents' names.

Figure 12-1

There were records in Hranice and Freiburg, including detailed police records and records in Yad Vashem showing, among other things, that some of the family had been in Theresienstadt. One of the Hranice records shows Josef working in Jagielnica, strengthening the case that this is where the family first lived.

There seemed to be no good lead to Sarah's parents with the exception of the Jewish names that appeared on some of the documents. The three eldest we know from the Jagielnica birth records. David, Anna, and Josef are probably direct translations. Moritz we learned was Moshe, and Gustav was Gabriel.

Breine Riss

It is hard to ignore the uncommon name Gabriel. The Skalat Pikholz families have two that I discussed in Chapter Eight, the possible son and great-grandson of Old Nachman. Two others died in infancy in 1850 and 1865. Another is mentioned in a marriage record that is so strange that I expect it is an error.

There is also Wilhelm Riss, born about 1860 with the given names Gabriel Wolf. His parents are Breine (sometimes Brane) Pikholz and Avraham Aron Riss. Breine's parents are Gabriel Riss and Ryfka Pikholz, a couple about whom we know nothing. Wilhelm is her first child, followed by Rifka (1862), Israel Yehudah (Isidor, 1866), Debora (1874), Moshe (Moses, 1876), Josef (1878) and Rosche (Rose, 1882).

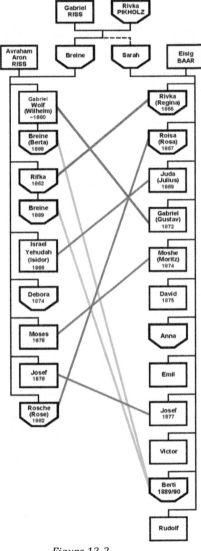

Figure 12-2

Wilhelm's daughter Berta was named Breine after her grandmother in 1888, and Rifka's daughter Breine was born in 1889. Rosche's eldest daughter Betty (1911) may also have been Breine, but Betty's American tombstone does not have her Jewish name. Moshe's daughter Bela may be Breine, but we have not found her family's graves in Cochabamba, Bolivia.

Wilhelm, Isidor, Josef, and Rosche have living descendants. Wilhelm has one living granddaughter in the United States, Isidor has two grandchildren (first cousins) in Europe, and Josef has a granddaughter in Israel and her two brothers in the United States. Rosche has a living daughter and four grandsons, all in the U.S.

There is nothing remarkable about two families with children named Rifka, Josef, Moshe, Juda, and Rosa. These are common names. But when both have a Gabriel and both name their first daughter Rifka, when we know that those are the mother's parents in one of the two families, it is hard not to consider that Sarah Baar might well be the younger sister of Breine Riss. Add to that Sarah's youngest daughter Berti, who was born about the same time as the two Riss girls named for their grandmother Breine.

No one that Milton and I spoke to had ever heard of the other family though some members of the families of the two Gabriels, Wilhelm and Gustav, had lived close enough to one another that they might well have.

Time for genetic genealogy

Milton was happy to do a Family Finder test. In fact, he ordered Y-37 and MtDNA tests as well. The other Baars were not interested.

I found two people to test on the Riss side, the first cousins Julia and one who prefers not to be named and whom I shall call "Mr. X", grandchildren of Isidor. I would like to have had some second cousins as well, but I take what I can get. In one of the families who declined to test, the mother asked me to be sure to let her know what I discover.

As both families are headed by women, putative sisters, a Y-DNA test would not be helpful. We have no candidates for MtDNA on the Baar side and only one on the Riss side who has not agreed to any contact. So the only option is Family Finder.

The mission is two-fold: a) to determine whether the DNA supports the idea of Breine Riss and Sarah Baar as sisters, and b) to see if there is any indication of their connection to other Pikholz families. I decided to separate the questions, first comparing the three amongst themselves.

		Total cM / Longest cM			Total Ranking (Pikholz ranking)		
		Milton	Julia	Mr.X	Milton	Julia	Mr.X
Suggested relationships	Milton	X	81/18	54/12	X	19 (5)	Distant (14)
	Julia	2-4 cousin	X	818/117	21 (9)	X	1 (1)
	Mr. X	4C - remote	1 cousin	X	Distant (14)	1 (1)	X

Figure 12-3

The first cousins Julia and Mr. X show up as first cousins. Each is the first match of the other. That is to be expected.

Their matches with Milton are not neat and tidy. If Breine and Sarah are sisters, Milton is a third cousin to Julia and Mr. X. That fits FTDNA's estimate of second-fourth cousins for Julia and Milton, but not Mr. X and Milton who are considered much more distant.

On the other hand, according to the wiki of the International Society of Genetic Genealogy (ISOGG), third cousins share 53.13 cM of DNA. That is almost precisely the match between Mr. X and Milton, with the match between Julia and Milton significantly closer.

Rebekah Canada writes in FTDNA's Frequently Asked Questions:

> *"As a result of frequent intermarriage, a Family Finder cousin match may show a total value of centiMorgans composed from the combination of different lines. That is, they are a more distant cousin who is related in multiple ways ...*
>
> *Beginning on April 21, 2011, we have modified our Family Finder matching algorithm to address this. The changes affect the match list for Ashkenazi Jews. The outcome is calculated Family Finder relationships that more accurately reflect relationships to other Ashkenazi Jews."*

But the FTDNA "secret formula" is not entirely appropriate here. Milton has only one Jewish grandparent, so he really does not need an endogamy adjustment. Julia and Mr. X have two Jewish grandparents—the ones that they share—so they also do not require much of an adjustment. Mr. X's 54 cM match with Milton looks to be what we want and with Julia's better match the outlier, a result of the randomness of DNA.

The other point of interest in these preliminary results is the fact that Milton has four Pikholz matches closer than Julia, and Julia has eight Pikholz matches closer than Milton. Considering what we know about the families, if Breine and Sarah are sisters no other Pikholz descendants can truly be closer than Milton and Julia are to each other. In fact, those better matches follow a distinct pattern.

Milton's first Pikholz matches are Uncle Bob; my cousins Lee and Herb; and Nan, the great-granddaughter of Moshe Hersch's son Berisch (see Chapter Six). Milton has two more suggested second-fourth Pikholz cousins after Julia—Charles and my cousin Rhoda.

Julia's first matches are Mr. X, Jane (Nan's cousin), my sister Judith, Charles, Herb, Leonora, Lee, and my sister Amy. Julia has two second-fourth Pikholz cousins after Milton—Nan and me.

The matches that Milton and Julia have before the match with each other are—for both of them—either in my own family or in the family of Moshe Hersch. Something significant is coming into focus.

Now having established that the total matches between Milton and Julia/Mr. X do not contradict the possibility that Breine and Sarah are sisters, we can proceed to look at the chromosomes.

Where Milton matches Julia and Mr. X

Before examining the chromosomes, let me mention again that this analysis suffers from the unwillingness—thus far—of the other Baar and Riss cousins to participate in this project. I hope that will change, and results from those additional cousins will strengthen our conclusions. Or perhaps bring it all crashing down.

The chromosome browser on FTDNA shows almost no matches for all three together. The only ones are on chromosomes 7 and 10 and both of those are small, to the point of insignificant.

> 3cM Matches for Milton
Top Julia
Bottom Mr. X

> 3cM Matches for Julia
Top Mr. X
Bottom Milton

> 3cM Matches for Mr. X
Top Julia
Bottom Milton

Figure 12-4

It appears that it may be easier to show Breine Riss and Sarah Baar to be sisters by their connections with other Pikholz families, rather than by identifying matches between the descendants of each.

How the families of Breine and Sarah match the other Pikholz families

I began with GEDmatch, omitting matches to the Rozdol descendants. My emphasis was on matches greater than 10 cM and occasionally on groups who match on over 5 cM. The numbers in parentheses are the sizes of the matches rounded to the closest cM.

Chromosome 1: Milton has a match with my third cousin, once removed Ralph (12). Julia has a large match with Leonora (25) and a group of matches with two of my sisters and me and my third cousin Joe (10) with a smaller match (7) in the same place with Aunt Betty.

Chromosome 2: Julia matches Leonora (19).

Chromosome 3: Milton matches Leonora (16). Mr. X has nearly congruent, small (6) matches with Aunt Betty, Uncle Bob, Herb, Leonora and my sister Amy.

Chromosome 4: Julia has small (6-7) but similar matches with Uncle Bob, Lee, three of my sisters and me. Mr. X has nearly congruent matches (18.5) with Aunt Betty and my cousin Marty and a smaller one (8) in the same place with Herb.

Chromosome 5: Julia has a large match (36) with Barbara, who you will meet in Chapter Thirteen, and smaller ones in the same place with Leonora and my cousin Rhoda. Mr. X has nearly congruent matches with Nan (24) and Barbara (21). These two matches do not triangulate on GEDmatch, but they do on FTDNA. I have no idea why that might be.

Chromosome 6: Julia has a set of small matches with Uncle Bob, Lee, two of my sisters, and me. Mr. X has a pair of matches (5.5) with Anna and her brother David, the descendants of Uncle Selig.

Chromosome 7: Milton has a match with Charles (17.5) and another with Leonora (10).

Chromosome 8: Julia has a match (11) with Bruce.

Chromosome 10: All three match Aunt Betty, Herb, and Leonora with medium sized matches. Mr. X has a small match with Anna and David.

Chromosome 11: Milton has large (32), nearly congruent matches with Uncle Bob and Lee, including segments that match Joe (18) and Herb (8.5). Julia has a match (15) with Gene.

Chromosome 12: Milton has a match with Herb (16) and Rhoda (18) and another with Herb alone (19). Julia has a match with Herb (13) and Lee (14) and a smaller one (7) with Aunt Betty, Uncle Bob and my sister Judith.

Chromosome 13: Milton has a match with Herb (15) and JudyT (19). Here too, they do not triangulate on GEDmatch but do on FTDNA. Julia has a match with Craig (10).

Chromosome 14: Julia has a large match (27) with Anna's brother David and another in the same place with Jane (14). Julia and Mr. X share a match with Barbara, Uncle Bob, and my sister Sarajoy.

Chromosome 16: Julia has matches with Jane, Nan, and Charles (13-18), a match that appears in Chapter Six. She also has a set of matches (8-9) with Aunt Betty, Uncle Bob and all four of my sisters. Mr. X has a match with Sarajoy (12).

Chromosome 17: Julia and Mr. X share matches with Lee, Barbara, my cousin Terry, and Filip. Some of those are more than 20 cM.

Chromosome 18: Milton has matches with me (12), Terry (10) and Herb (8), all in the same place. Mr. X has nearly identical matches (10) with Uncle Bob, Herb, Amy, Sarajoy and me.

Chromosome 19: Milton has overlapping matches with Anna (16) and JudyT (11) and another with Dalia (11). Mr. X has a match with Leonora (11).

Chromosome 20: Milton has a match with Nan (22) which includes a match with Jane (16). Mr. X overlaps both of those. Milton also has matches (21-30) with Herb, Uncle Bob, and my sisters Amy and Jean. Julia has large matches with Jane (36), Lloyd (36), and Charles (34), which overlap smaller matches with Nan (13) and Leonora (13). Julia has another set of matches (10-11.4) with Jane, Nan, Leonora, and Dalia.

Chromosome 21: Milton has a match with JudyT (14), and Julia has a match with Marty (18).

Chromosome 22: Julia has a set of matches with my sisters Jean and Judith (24), Herb (22), Amy (19), and me (17). She also has a match with Gene (11.5). Mr. X has a match with Dalia (12) which he shares partially with Julia.

These results are particularly well-focused. Almost all of the matches between the Riss and Baar families are with either my own family or with the Moshe Hersch descendants Nan, Jane, Charles, and Leonora. There is also some representation of the descendants of Uncle Selig. There are very few matches of interest with descendants of either Old Nachman or Peretz Pikholz—or for that matter with Vladimir or Joyce. What unifies the matches here is they are all descendants of Isak Josef Pikholz. So is JudyT, through Isak Josef's son Berl. There are a few matches with Dalia, Barbara, and Lloyd, but those descendants of Mordecai and Taube may also be descendants of Isak Josef.

Normally it would be an easy next step to postulate that Rifka Pikholz, the mother of Breine Riss and (apparently) Sarah Baar, is a daughter of Isak Josef. However, we already know that my great-great-grandmother Rivka Feige is the daughter of Isak Josef, so he could not have had a daughter Rifka as well!

That appears to leave one possibility. Figure 12-5 is the birth record for Breine's children Moses and Debora. The record is dated 13 December 1888 and states that Moses and Debora were born in 1874 and 1876. Less than two months later, on 5 February 1889, a daughter Breine was born to Breine's daughter Rifka. So we know that Breine Riss was dead by then, very likely even before 13 December 1888. That record says that Breine's parents are Gabriel Riss and Ryfka Pikholz, but it may not be entirely accurate. Breine's husband Gabriel was named for by 1860, and Breine herself may well not have been the one to provide her mother's name. Breine's parents are not named in any other document in our possession.

Figure 12-5

The scenario that suggests itself is this. Gabriel and Ryfka had two daughters, Breine and Sarah, in the early to mid-1840s. Gabriel died when the daughters were young, perhaps very young. Ryfka, the young widow, then married her (indeterminate) cousin Isak Fischel, with whom she had four more children—the youngest my great-grandfather Hersch. The 1888 record marking the births of Breine's children Moses and Debora does not have Ryfka's second name Feige, perhaps because the person providing the information did not know the full name.

Our ability to analyze Family Finder tests does not include the level of precision necessary for drawing this kind of conclusion. As Sherlock Holmes said to Dr. Watson, "How often have I said to you that when you have eliminated the impossible, whatever remains, however improbable, must be the truth?"

I cannot really draw hard conclusions based on the little I have to work with. The only thing I can draw is a broken line showing Ryfka and Rivka Feige to be perhaps the same person. But I think this is right. My great-great-grandmother Rivka Feige was previously married to Gabriel Riss, and Milton, Julia, and Mr. X are my half-third cousins.

Chapter Thirteen

Simon and Barbara

Descendants

Simon Pikholz and his wife Dwore Waltuch had two known daughters, Lea and Breine. Lea gave birth to twelve children from 1882 to 1906. The first nine were born in Kopicienice (east Galicia) and the last three in Czernovitz, where Lea died in 1913. Breine was born in January 1860 and her paper trail ends there.

Dwore herself died in Skalat in October 1861 at age twenty-three, so we can guess that Simon was probably born in the mid-1830s.

Left with two babies, Simon married his late wife's sister Chana (b. ~1848) and they appear to have had eight or nine children over twenty-two years beginning in 1863. Four of those children went to the United States, and at least three have living descendants as does Lea, the older sister from the first wife.

There is no information on Simon himself. He is not seen entering the U.S., so it is likely that he died before Chana left Skalat in 1892. His sons' names are Marcus, Herz, and Jossel Leisor. Herz is Chana's father. Marcus is probably Mordecai who could be Simon's father, but this is not much in the way of evidence.

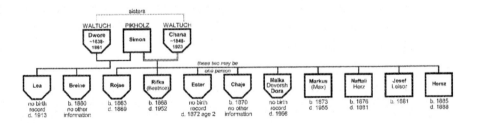

Figure 13-1

There is a bit of confusion in the records of this family. Rojse's death record gives her age as 24, when she is in fact nearly 26. Chaje and Ester seem to be the same person even though the birth and death records have different names. Dora's Jewish name Malka Devorah appears on her New Jersey tombstone, and July 1872 is the birth date recorded for Social Security. However, there is no birth record, so neither the birth date nor the birth name can be considered confirmed. Max used 1878 as his birth year in the U.S. though the 1873 birth record seems to be his. And Jossel Leisor—Joseph in the U.S.—disappears entirely a few years after the birth of his fourth child.

Simon himself signs his name (misspelled) as Shimon in Hebrew letters, so there is little doubt about his Jewish name though it is not clear that it appears in subsequent generations. Lea had eight sons, at least four born after Simon died, but none seem to be named for him. Max has one son, and his tombstone says "Shlomo" (=Solomon). But a living cousin says that he was called "Shimmy" by the family, so the stone is probably wrong. Joseph's elder son is Sam, but his stone has no Hebrew lettering. Dora's second son Sam's Jewish name is Shalom, not Shimon. Beatrice had only daughters and granddaughters.

There is one bit of information that suggests a specific connection to another Pikholz family. When the parents of Charles (see Chapter Six) went from Vienna to the United States in 1939, his mother's visa application stated that she would be joining her "distant cousin" Samuel in Elizabeth, New Jersey. This Samuel we know as the son of Dora, the same Sam whose Jewish name is Shalom.

If Charles' great-grandfather Szulim (=Shalom) and Simon are brothers, Dora's son Sam might have been named in 1906 for his grandfather's brother, even though a second cousin is not what we would normally call "distant." There is a Skalat record for the 1897 death of Szulim Pikholz, age 53, but there is no assurance that this Szulim is Charles' great-grandfather, though 1844 would be about right for his birth.

Both parents of Charles' maternal grandmother have the surname Pikholz, and we do not know the connection between them. So being related to Charles on his Pikholz side carries a bit of ambiguity. That ambiguity goes double and more for Charles' second cousin Leonora, whose mother Taube, has four Pikholz grandparents.

It is also worth noting that when Dora went to the U.S. in 1891 she traveled with Sara Frankel, a Pikholz descendant who is a first cousin of my grandfather. This may imply a cousinhood between the two young women, or it may simply be two nineteen-year olds from the same town who happen to be distant cousins. In any event, I have seen nothing that would allow for them to have been closer than second cousins and even that is far from certain.

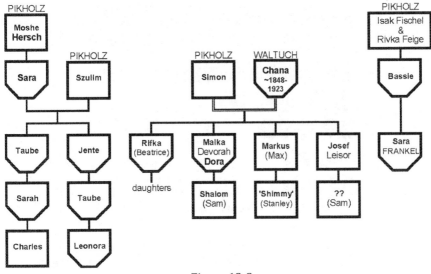

Figure 13-2

Barbara

As usual, we turn to DNA to see whether there is anything we might learn. The sole male-line descendant of Simon is the grandson of Max. He has not consented to testing, so we cannot confirm that Simon himself is a male-line Pikholz descendant. Josef Leisor has one biological grandchild, but he has a very common name and we have no contact with him or his four children. Beatrice has one living granddaughter, but neither she nor Beatrice's four great-grandchildren have been willing to test.

That leaves Dora's family where Sam has one daughter, and his brother has a daughter and a son. Sam's daughter Barbara agreed to do a Family Finder test.

Barbara's second closest of some four thousand matches is Charles, who FTDNA estimates as a second-third cousin. Her closest match is a Pikholz descendant named Lloyd, a descendant of Mordecai.

Barbara has nine matches with Pikholz descendants who are estimated to be second-fourth cousins. Those include Leonora, Dalia, six members of my own family, and Nan's daughter. Nan herself is a slightly more distant match to

Barbara, suggesting that Nan's daughter's connection is partly on her father's side.

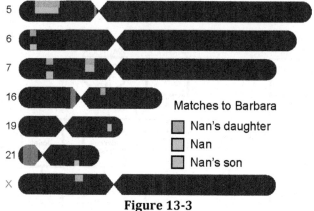

Figure 13-3

On chromosomes 5 and 7, Nan and her daughter match Barbara together. But the matches that Nan's children share with Barbara on chromosomes 6, the left side of 7, 16, 21, and X must be from Nan's husband's side. We are all one family, all one people.

Barbara also has third-fifth cousin matches with David Dekel (Chapter Eight), one of my second cousins, one Rozdoler, and Nan. Finally, Barbara has more distant matches with fourteen other Pikholz descendants, including four Rozdolers. She has no matches with my Kwoczka cousins.

The chromosomes

The important thing, as usual, is how GEDmatch shows the matches on Barbara's individual chromosomes. That is where the patterns can show themselves. Here are the most interesting, all of them checked for triangulation.

Chromosome 1 features matches with Charles (21.6 cM) and me (15.5 cM) on a segment where Charles and I have a match of 40.6 cM.

Chromosome 3 has a set of nearly congruent matches in the 6-6.5 cM range with Leonora, Uncle Selig's great-granddaughter Anna, and four of my family.

Chromosome 5 shows a match of 10.5 cM with Leonora, which includes a match of 6 cM with my cousin Rhoda.

Chromosome 6 has overlapping matches with Bruce and Bonnie, both descendants of Peretz Pikholz (b. 1820). The same chromosome has a 6.6 cM segment shared by Nan's cousin Jane and my cousin Terry.

Chromosome 8 has nearly congruent matches of over 10 cM with my two Jaffe cousins on my mother's side. That's another example of everyone-is-related-to-everyone endogamy.

The main feature on chromosome 10 is Barbara's match of 43.5 cM with Charles.

On chromosome 13, Barbara has a match of 20.5 cM with Leonora containing a matching segment of 7.7 cM with Charles. That should be a simple enough observation, as we know that Charles and Leonora are cousins. But it isn't. Charles and Leonora do not match on chromosome 13, so triangulation fails. Barbara matches one on her father's side—where we would expect both of them to be—and one on her mother's side. This too is endogamy, one example of many in Barbara's matches.

Barbara's mother is from Zhvanets in Podolia about 65 miles from Skalat, yet, typical of European Jews and the "failed" triangulations show she has a number of matches with Pikholz descendants—aside from with Barbara herself. If we had tests from even one or two of Barbara's first and second cousins, cousins who are not related to Barbara's mother, we might be able to clarify some of this.

Chr 14

Match ID	Type	Name	Matching segments on Chromosome 14
1	F2	*Pikholz - Sarajoy	25434780 - 41907596 (22.8787 cM)
2	F2	*Pikholz - Uncle Bob	25548001 - 41907596 (22.5972 cM)
3	F2	*Pikholz - Aunt Betty	23256061 - 36427163 (23.4524 cM)
4	F2	*Pikholz - Israel	23265976 - 35753530 (22.6836 cM)
5	F2	*Pikholz - Terry	23208117 - 32646188 (16.9129 cM)
6	F2	*Pikholz - Lee	23273635 - 28168024 (7.2112 cM, 32600306 - 33922869 (4.4793 cM)

Chr 14

Figure 13-4

On chromosome 14, we have an interesting case. Barbara matches my aunt and uncle, my sister Sarajoy, and me in overlapping segments of 22.5-23.5

cM. Included in that are segments where Barbara matches my second cousins Terry (16.9 cM) and Lee (7.2 cM). The important match here is Barbara and Terry. Lee is my double second cousin. Our grandfathers are brothers and our grandmothers are sisters. So without Terry, Barbara matches five of us who are related on both my grandfather's side and my grandmother's side. The fact that Terry matches here as well shows that the entire matching segment is Pikholz DNA, not some hitherto unknown connection between Barbara and my grandmother's Hungarian or Slovakian ancestors.

Again, note that on the chromosome browsers provided by both FTDNA and GEDmatch, the bars that represent the matching segments are not proportional. Longer bars can represent shorter segments and vice versa.

On chromosome 15, there is a large segment of 47.8 cM matching Lloyd. This segment appears to include eight other segments of interest. But, in fact, it only triangulates with Bruce and Bonnie. The others—Jane, Vladimir, Charles, Uncle Bob, Sarajoy, and I—do not match Lloyd on chromosome 15. The one interesting triangulation is that Barbara, Jane, and Vladimir all match in the same place. Here too, Lloyd, Bruce, and Bonnie match Barbara via one of her parents while the rest match her through the other parent.

Chr 15

Match ID	Type	Name	Matching segments on Chromosome 15
1	F2	*Pikholz - Lloyd	45773904 - 87254866 (47.8247 cM)
2	F2	*Pikholz - Bruce	44664740 - 48453732 (3.4669 cM) 66547489 - 72220030 (7.3045 cM)
3	F2	*Pikholz - Jane	57571940 - 64111266 (7.6882 cM)
4	F2	*Pikholz - Vladimir	57504379 - 63453712 (6.7333 cM)
5	F2	*Pikholz - Charles	60998928 - 65078336 (5.0937 cM)
6	F2	*Pikholz - Uncle Bob	79014013 - 82470162 (37597 cM)
7	F2	*Pikholz - Bonnie	76317892 - 80342297 (6.6365 cM)
8	F2	*Pikholz - Israel	73247816 - 771108572 (3.0786 cM)
9	F2	*Pikholz - Sarajoy	73247816 - 771108572 (3.0786 cM)

Chr 14

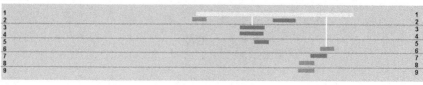

Figure 13-5

112

Another non-triangulating group appears on chromosome 17 where Barbara matches Charles over 12.9 cM, but Charles does not match Barbara's matches with my family on the same segment.

Chromosome 20 shows Barbara with matches of 18-23.5 cM with Dalia, Leonora, and my father's cousin Herb; all nicely triangulated. Someone in Pikholz history was an ancestor of all four.

Chr 20

Match ID	Type	Name	Matching segments on Chromosome 20
1	F2	*Pikholz - Herb	11138257 - 35306609 (23.2658 cM)
2	F2	*Pikholz - Leomora	11186791 - 34911766 (22.8078 cM)
3	F2	*Pikholz - Dalia	14266619 - 34474702 (18.2498 cM)

Chr 20

Figure 13-6

These are what seem to me to be the most interesting parts of Barbara's autosomal matches.

Barbara's Main Matches

Chromosome	Family Finder matches	Likely common ancestor
1	Charles & Israel	Unknown
3	Leonora, Anna, my family	Izak Josef (1784)
5	Leonora & Rhoda	Izak Josef or Mordecai
6	Bruce, Bonnie, Jane, Terry	Someone ancient (endogamy)
10	Charles (43.5 cM)	Unknown
13	Charles Leonora	Unknown Izak Josef or Mordecai
14	My family	Izak Josef or Mordecai
15	Lloyd, Bruce, Bonnie Jane, Charles, Vladimir, my family	Unknown Izak Josef (except Vladimir)
20	Leonora, Dalia, Herb	Mordecai

Figure 13-7

The question remains, who are Simon's parents? It is risky to speculate based on Barbara's DNA alone. Her grandmother, Dora, inherited different segments from Simon than did her sister Beatrice and brothers Max and

Joseph. Further, the DNA that Barbara received from Dora is not the same as what her first cousins received. But even so, it is worth doing the exercise.

Among the Skalat Pikholz lines that go back to the early 1800s—Isak Josef (1784), Nachman (1795), Mordecai (1805), Moshe Hersch (1810s), Isak Fischel (~1820) and Peretz (1820)—we can probably eliminate Nachman as his descendants have no significant matches with Barbara.

We have determined that Isak Fischel's wife, Rivka Feige, is the daughter of Isak Josef. I would not be surprised if Mordecai's wife Taube is also a daughter of Isak Josef. What would really surprise me would be if I could find some actual evidence of that. As I wrote back in Chapter Six, my analysis of Jane's DNA matches gave me the impression that her great-great-grandfather Moshe Hersch might be the brother of Mordecai. If Taube was indeed the daughter of Isak Josef, then I would suggest that Jane's Moshe Hersch is Taube's brother, not Mordecai's.

Leonora has DNA from Isak Josef and double DNA from Mordecai on her grandfather's side. Because of the match with Anna (Uncle Selig's great-great-granddaughter) and my great-great-grandmother, the segment on chromosome 3 appears definitely to be from Isak Josef. If Moshe Hersch is the son of Isak Josef as I suspect, then the second segment of chromosome 15 is also from Isak Josef.

The segment on chromosome 20 is from Mordecai/Taube.

If we were able to say with confidence that Charles' great-grandfather Szulim (a likely brother of Simon) is the son of Mordecai, then the question of Simon's parents would be settled.

In any event, Simon is a descendant of both Mordecai and Isak Josef and how that lines up is not clear at all. Thus far, we do not see Simon with obvious multiple Pikholz ancestors. To complicate matters further, I have been assuming that Isak Josef and Mordecai are brothers, or father and son, or uncle and nephew, or at least close cousins. I could display a dozen scenarios and not be certain that I had included the correct one.

This is the problem of recent endogamy, and we would probably not be able to come close to a solution even if all of Barbara's first and second cousins were to test.

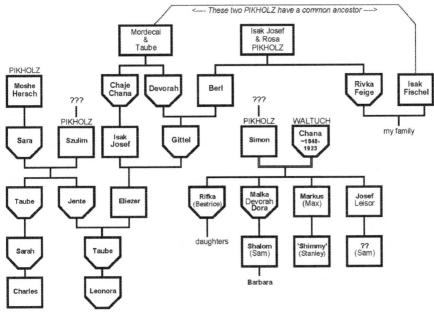

Figure 13-8

Chapter Fourteen

What Does This Prove?

When non-alcoholics speak of "proof," they are usually talking about science, or mathematics or logic or the law. Much as we like to think otherwise, proof is often not absolute. The very fact that the term "absolute proof" is not a redundancy reminds us that proof is not automatically absolute. We can say the same thing about "truth."

In science, the truth is whatever the consensus of the day has accepted, and it remains so until it is successfully challenged. Scientific authorities tell us that this or that food is good for you (or bad for you) until some later scientific authority "proves" otherwise. This is as it should be, as science is about challenging accepted truths. Without it, there could be no progress. But since science examines the real world, it is hard to get away from the idea that there is an actual, real, absolute truth out there waiting to be discovered and announced to the world.

In mathematics, everyone knows that the shortest distance between two points is a straight line, but whenever anyone said that in earshot of my father he would say "on a plane." This truth, that everyone knows, is limited to a very particular set of conditions—in this case the two-dimensional world that we do not inhabit.

The law often speaks of "proof beyond a reasonable doubt," a term which itself bears witness to the existence of some superior proof that is beyond any doubt whatsoever. Our instincts tell us that the legal or criminal event in question either happened or did not, and the circumstances are one of those advocated by one of the parties or perhaps others that no party "knows" fully. The attorneys advocate for the adversarial parties, and the judge or jury decides what truth will be recorded for posterity. Or at least until appeal.

James Tanner, a genealogist who blogs at *Genealogy's Star*[1] and has a background as a trial attorney, wrote a series of three blogs on this subject in September 2014. He begins his second part with:

> *"Do we really want genealogists to be lawyers and judges? Some genealogists seem bound and determined to convert what is essentially a historical investigation into a branch of the law."*

He continues in his third part with:

"On the other hand, there is also a significant segment of the genealogical community that are [sic] devoted to the "scientific method" as applied to genealogy. Those promoting scientific genealogical research speak in terms of proposing a hypothesis, developing a theory and examining the evidence to support the theory."

And:

"There are even those who would support a middle ground that incorporates terminology and methodology from both science and law."

James does not approve. Neither do I.

Family genealogy is the pursuit by a single person or a small group in search of the history of a particular family using traditional documents, personal testimonies and recollections, photographs, tombstones and other artifacts in order to best reconstruct the family history. The basic facts exist even when the researcher does not have access to them. But there are no answers "in the back of the book." And there is no judge or jury or peer-review committee to decide if the conclusions drawn from the research pass muster.

The researcher is often confronted with documents that contradict one another or documents that do not conform to personal testimony. The researcher must decide if it matters whether Aunt Ethel was born on the twenty-ninth of August or the first of September, once it is clear that both documents refer to the same person. And whether it matters or not, something has to go in the space marked "birth date" with the rest of the debate in the "comments" section.

It is more complicated when there may be more than one person involved. There is a Skalat death record for fifty-nine year old Mordecai Pikholz in 1864. That is the basis for all my references in this book to Mordecai's birth year as 1805. But in fact, there is nothing on that death record that ties that particular Mordecai to the Mordecai whose Y-DNA matches my own. The first known descendant to carry Mordecai's name was born in 1867, but that is not dispositive. In my Brother's Keeper database, I have them as two different people with notes that say they are probably the same person. But since I believe them to be the same person, my website, and any written descriptions proceed on the assumption that they are.

Eastern European Jewish research suffers—as do any number of other groups—from a lack of records at critical times. So we do the best we can. If we are responsible genealogists, we note all the problematic issues. For if I am the family genealogist, others will assume that I have done the work, and whatever I say is true. In fact, once I write it, I myself will rarely revisit the issue.

In the end, for my projects, I decide just as you, dear reader, will decide for your projects. Perhaps some family member will look over your shoulder, but the decisions are subjective and are not subject to review by someone holding "the truth" in his pocket. Your family members may review your decision as a jury or a peer-review committee, but unless they have been withholding information or documents their word is no better that yours.

I have written and spoken on the subject of what to do when you know something but the documentation just isn't there. My mantras have become "If it may be wrong, it doesn't belong" and "If there is an 85 percent chance that something is so, there is a 15 percent chance that it is 100 percent wrong." My policy has become when you are certain of something but do not have the documents to verify it, get one more piece of supporting evidence before accepting it.

Except in specific cases, DNA cannot prove anything useful. In this book, I have largely avoided the word "prove," preferring the word "demonstrate." It is true that a Y-DNA test or an MtDNA test can prove that there exists a common ancestor, but it cannot tell us much about whether the ancestor that Zachy and I share is six or seven generations previous or even further back. DNA can prove that Zachy and I do not share a male-line common ancestor with Vladimir. Important though this is, this particular finding is of limited value.

Autosomal DNA can prove parent-child and sibling relationships, but once you get to the cousins, it is not sufficient. I did a brief consultation for a woman who wanted to identify her father.

She had taken an autosomal test that showed her to be a probable niece to a particular man and a probable first cousin to the son and daughter of two of his three deceased brothers. The implication was clear and obvious that by simple process of elimination her father was brother number four, who had never married and had no known children.

At first blush, this was all the proof that she could hope for, and all she needed was for someone to tell her it is indeed correct. I couldn't do that. "How do you know," I asked her, "that there was not another brother out there somewhere that no one knew of? Perhaps one born before the parents were married and given up for adoption." She was not asking for something to "demonstrate" that brother number four was her father. She wanted proof, and it wasn't there. I suggested that she acquire some of his possessions, because maybe in a few years the testing companies will be able to work with hat bands, hair brushes and the like to retrieve DNA from the dead.

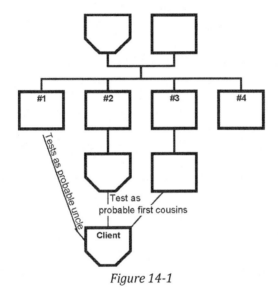

Figure 14-1

DNA cannot stand alone as a determining factor. It can and often does support research or give new direction to research that has run aground. Autosomal DNA can give me a strong indication that there is one Moshe Hersch, but not much beyond that. It can play a key role in identifying the descendants of Uncle Selig. It could help determine if we can cross the double traffic light from Old Nachman's family to David Dekel's family. It can demonstrate the Riss-Baar connection beyond the parallel given names and open a new possibility regarding the relationship between my great-great-grandparents, Rivka Feige and Isak Fischel. And it can help make sense of the intertwining Mordecai-Isak Josef family structure.

Autosomal DNA and the tools developed to analyze it allow us to construct partial genomes of past generations and to use those to draw at least tentative conclusions about relationships among those long gone.

But by and large, autosomal DNA is not proof. It can help draw broken or dotted lines between people on our tree charts, but without significant supporting evidence, it cannot allow us to draw solid lines. It's really wrong to say "DNA... without significant supporting evidence," because it is usually the DNA which comes to support a structure of evidence that pre-exists the test.

In the following chapters, we will go further into the deep weeds of autosomal DNA and the type of conclusions we can draw from it. Let us see what else we can demonstrate.

---

[1] Actually, James Tanner maintains a whole string of blogs. This is the one I follow as best as I can keep up.

Chapter Fifteen

Genes from My Father

Kitty Cooper's mapping tools

I took an evening break from the program at the 34th IAJGS International Conference on Jewish Genealogy held in the summer of 2014 in Salt Lake City. During that break, I met for two and a half hours with Kitty Munson Cooper, one of the tech gurus of genetic genealogy. Gaye Tannenbaum, a DNA-adoption Search Angel and adoption activist[1], participated as well.

I knew Kitty had developed tools that map chromosome segments for the purpose of determining which parts of a person's DNA came from which ancestors. Assuming I am talking about my own ancestors, the first step is to look at my matches with all my known relatives. This is similar to the chromosome browser provided by FTDNA but is not limited to five matches at a time like at FTDNA. Kitty's *Chromosome Mapper* can handle up to twenty matching relatives.

FTDNA's chromosome browser has an option to show the results in a csv file (something very similar to Excel). You do that for your first five matches, then add to it the next five matches and so on until you have all the relatives you want for the *Chromosome Mapper*. You put that csv file into the *Chromosome Mapper* and it shows the matches as on the FTDNA chromosome browser, but with more lines and more colors.

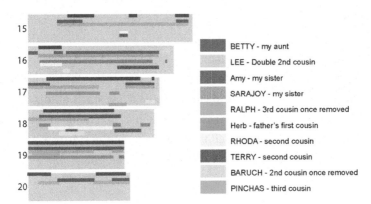

Figure 15-1

You then do a visual inspection of the *Chromosome Mapper* results to determine which segments come from which ancestor or ancestral couple and add that information manually into the csv file. This modified csv file is then fed into Kitty's second tool, the *Segment Mapper*, to produce a chart showing which ancestors contributed which segments to my DNA. The *Segment Mapper* can handle up to forty ancestors or ancestral couples.

Figure 15-2 shows what parts of my own chromosomes 15-20 appear to come from which of my father's ancestors.

Figure 15-2

The *Segment Mapper* was fine for what it was, but I wanted something else. I wanted to turn it upside down, not to see what DNA came from which ancestors or ancestral couples but to show if I could reconstruct the DNA of some of those ancestors based on the DNA of their descendants. I felt that if I could identify enough segments as having come from a particular couple I could see which other Pikholz families (or Pikholz wannabes, as in Chapter Eleven) carry some of those same segments.

That would require using not only my matches with my relatives but their matches with each other that didn't include me, all the time taking care to avoid possible false matches due to endogamy. I made a few starts at this, but it was simpler in theory than in fact. It was not enough to do standard triangulation based on three or more people all matching one another. It was as though I needed a more complex, specifically Jewish triangulation,

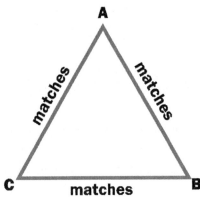

TRIANGULATION:
Where

A

matches

matches

C   matches   B

JEWISH
TRIANGULATION:

Where everyone
matches everyone

Kitty Cooper herself picked up on the idea of using the *Segment Mapper* in reverse. She used the colors to show which combination of descendants led to the inclusion of which segments. Some were based on as many as six or seven matching descendants, but most used only two or three.

I was not going to work with segments based on only two matches, and in any case, I had more outstanding tests that I wanted to incorporate into my own study before proceeding. I was convinced, however, that this was the way to go in trying to connect the Pikholz families in the early 1800s to one another and the families in the later 1800s to the earlier ones.

Lazarus—My father

Before I had a chance to get back to this, GEDmatch came out with a tool called "*Lazarus*," which allows users to create "pseudo-DNA kits" based on matches among family members. These kits can then be used as surrogates for deceased or otherwise unavailable ancestors.

Creating a *Lazarus* kit requires two groups of relatives of the deceased. Group 1 is descendants of the deceased. Group 2 is other genetic relatives of the deceased, but not descendants. Any segment which is common to both groups is considered a segment that the deceased had. If you reverse Group 1 and Group 2, the results should remain exactly the same, though for some reason sometimes they do not.

GEDmatch offers the results in three forms. For a "trial run," no kit is produced. They just show you the results that are then discarded. "No batch processing" produces a kit that is saved and can be used for "one-to-one" comparisons. "Full processing" produces a kit that can be used in a "one-to-many" comparison, just as any real kit can.

The results of *Lazarus* show all the matches between the members of both groups above the threshold you set—the default being 6 cM. It can be set as low as 4 cM or as high as 15 cM.

The great value in using Lazarus rather than Kitty Cooper's Segment Mapper is that it is simple and automatic. That is also its weak point, particularly for endogamous families. You cannot examine segments and weed out the ones that do not seem right. Nor can you say that you want more than just one match from each group in order to accept a segment.

I decided that before trying something too ambitious, I would attempt to "Lazarize" my father. When I first tried this, I had test results from two of my sisters, but now as I write there are results from all four. So Group 1 had three members in the first iteration and five later. This gave me the opportunity to see how much the fourth and fifth descendants added to the results.

There are quite a few candidates for Group 2, genetic non-descendant relatives of my father, starting with his sister, brother, and first cousin Herb. In addition, there are my four second cousins on the Pikholz side. There are also two cousins on my father's paternal grandmother's (Kwoczka) side—Baruch, my father's second cousin, and Pinchas, the son of another of my father's second cousins. There are a son, a daughter, and a grandson of three of my father's Pikholz second cousins. All these appear in Appendix A.

Finally, there are two on my grandmother's side—Shabtai, a second cousin of my father's on my great-grandmother's side, and Fred, the son of a half-first cousin on my great-grandfather's side. Fred has only one Jewish grandparent. See those cousins in Appendix B.

Of the fourteen candidates for my father's Group 2, only Aunt Betty, Uncle Bob, and Fred appear to be reliably free of possible Jewish matches from some non-relevant ancestor. Herb and my double second cousin Lee would have some endogamous effect. The other nine would have at least two Jewish ancestral lines not shared by my father.

I decided to experiment, using two or four of my sisters (plus my own kit) in Group 1 and various combinations in Group 2. The idea was to determine how much of my father's kit I could recreate using only very close family with no endogamous component and how much would that increase as I added more relatives who might also introduce false, endogamous matches.

The results, which exclude the X chromosome, were better than I expected.

GROUP 1	G R O U P 2	Total cM	of total
3	A.Betty, U.Bob, Fred	3286.3	45.8%
5	A.Betty, U.Bob, Fred	3412.8	47.6%
5	A.Betty, U.Bob	3360.3	46.8%
5	A.Betty, U.Bob, Fred, Herb, Lee	3532.9	49.2%
5	A.Betty, U.Bob, 12 others	3566.7	49.7%

Figure 15-3

How ever I tried it, the resulting *Lazarus* kit for my father was more than forty-five percent complete.[2] Using five descendants instead of three descendants added about one percent. In Group 2, Fred added a bit less than one percent. Herb and Lee, with one non-related family, added less than two percent. The nine other cousins with two or more non-related lines added less than one percent.

So clearly, I could work with "my father's kit" at a reasonably high level without worrying about possibly having introduced false segments. Keep in mind that according to the GEDmatch wiki, "Created kits must contain at least 1500 cM total segment length before they will be eligible for batch processing. Smaller kits may be used only for one-to-one matches." So by that measurement, any version of my father's kit must be considered a success.

My father's parents

It was clear that a kit for my paternal grandfather would be more of a challenge. Aunt Betty and Uncle Bob would move to Group 1, putting a total of seven there because they are his descendants. Fred and Shabtai would leave Group 2 because they are on my grandmother's side, so I would need to use more people with non-related family lines. Lee would become particularly problematic because he is on both my grandfather's side and my grandmother's side. Lee's DNA would definitely be creating false matches from a Pikholz/Kwoczka perspective.

GROUP 1	G R O U P 2	Total cM	of total
7	Herb	2006.5	28.0%
7	Herb, Terry, Rhoda, Marty, Lee	3124.6	43.6%
7	Herb, Terry, Rhoda, Marty	2785.1	38.8%
7	Add two Kwoczka cousins	2949.2	41.1%
7	Add three more Pikholz cousins	3039.5	42.4%

Figure 15-4

Herb is the only Group 2 candidate with only one non-Pikholz line, his father's. But a kit for my grandfather on this basis would not even be 30 percent complete. We get a much fuller kit by adding my second cousins, but Lee has significant matches with Group 1 based on our grandmothers' side, so I should really leave him out. My grandfather's Kwoczka and Pikholz cousins would add a bit more, but there is no telling how much of that might be false due to the endogamy introduced by the spouses of my grandfather's aunts and uncle.

So if I wanted to use my grandfather's kit for anything, I would use a kit made of Group 2 comprised of Herb, Terry, Rhoda, and Marty. The resulting 2785.1 cM is still well beyond the GEDmatch threshold of 1500 cM.

A kit for my grandmother is easy, but weak. Group 1 is her two children and five grandchildren, just as my grandfather's kit. But only Fred, the grandson of her half-sister, and Shabtai, the son of her first cousin, qualify for her Group 2. Lee qualifies, but would certainly introduce Pikholz endogamy, so I cannot use his kit responsibly. The resulting kit is only 958.8 cM, barely one eighth complete and well below the GEDmatch threshold of 1500 cM necessary for batch processing.

What will be interesting will be applying this technique to my great-grandparents.

---

[1] Adoption Search Angel—someone who uses available resources (particularly online resources) to reconnect those separated by adoption, donor conceived people, and just plain old "don't know who my father was."
DNA Search Angel—Adoption Search Angel with specific expertise in genetic genealogy.
Adoption Activist—A person who advocates for the restoration of rights to sealed records in adoption cases, specifically the original birth record or birth certificate. Activities include lobbying state legislators, commenting online on articles dealing with restoration of access (there are currently several active bills in various U.S. state legislatures including New York, Pennsylvania, Indiana, and Missouri), writing opinion pieces, and organizing political demonstrations.

² There is some debate about the total number of centiMorgans in the twenty-two pairs of human autosomal chromosomes. GEDmatch shows 3587 cM, which you can see by comparing a kit to itself.

The wiki of the International Society of Genetic Genealogy (ISOGG) uses 6766.2 cM for the two sets of chromosomes, which is 3383.1 cM each. (See http://www.isogg.org/wiki/Autosomal_DNA_statistics.) That is almost six percent less than what GEDmatch uses. But ISOGG itself is not much concerned with precision, as they round up to 6800 cM for convenience.

Chapter Sixteen

The Recreation of the Great-Grandparents

My father's paternal grandparents

After reconstructing much of the DNA of my father and grandfather, it is time to move on to the next generation—my great-grandparents. The way I see it, if I can substantially recreate the genes of each of my great-grandparents I can then examine how other people match them and perhaps draw some tentative conclusions about the relationships. This could be particularly helpful for non-Pikholz descendants who match many Pikholz kits—the kind I discussed in Chapter Eleven.

This is no simple matter. First of all, although I have a dozen descendants of Hersch and Jute Leah Pickholz who would go into Group 1, the matter of Group 2, genetically related non-descendants, is a problem. In the case of my great-grandmother, there are kits for only two such cousins, Baruch and Pinchas. Baruch, who I discussed in Chapter Three, is a second cousin of my father; his grandfather Rachmiel Kwoczka is the younger brother of my Jute Leah. Pinchas is my third cousin; his great-grandfather and namesake Pinchas Kwoczka is Jute Leah's other, probably older, brother. That means that the DNA we can identify as belonging to Jute Leah is limited to the matches that these two cousins have with the dozen in Group 1.

The descendants of my great-grandparents appear in Appendix A with Baruch and Pinchas on the far right, and the Pikholz third cousins on the far left.

Group 2 for my great-grandfather Hersch Pickholz is more problematic. We have Joe, a great-grandson of Hersch's sister Bassie, and we have Elaine and Ralph, a great-granddaughter and a great-great-grandson of Hersch's sister Leah. We also have more distant cousins who were discussed in some detail in previous chapters. And let us not forget that Hersch's parents, Rivka Feige and Isak Fischel, are both Pikholz.

Endogamy will play a major role in this analysis—not because these other cousins will introduce distant ancestral DNA into the Lazarus model to gum up the works, but because they will introduce more recent endogamy from what appear to be multiple marriages between Isak Josef's family and Mordecai and Taube's family. Mordecai, readers may recall, is a close, though indeterminate relative of Hersch's father Isak Fischel. Isak Josef is the father of Hersch's mother Rivka Feige.

The Kwoczka endogamy is probably the more traditional type. Some distant ancestral DNA from the non-Kwoczka side of the cousins, Baruch and Pinchas, may have come to us from our non-Kwoczka sides whether Pikholz or otherwise.

There is also a technical problem. GEDmatch allows only ten people in Group 1, and Hersch and Jute Leah have twelve descendants who have taken Family Finder tests. My first instinct would be to omit two of my sisters since we are five, but as you will see that is not the best way to go.

Jute Leah Kwoczka

In this kind of analysis, there is a certain tension between trying to include as many people as possible in order to uncover the maximum number of matching segments yet excluding those cousins who are most likely to introduce false DNA into the reconstituted ancestor.

An example of that is my second cousin Lee, whom I left out of the Lazarus kits of my grandparents (in Chapter Fifteen) because he is related to both of them.

In the case of Jute Leah, the problem is my second cousin Rhoda. Her contribution to the family project is significant, but not for this particular analysis.

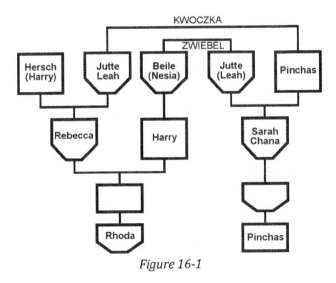

Figure 16-1

Resulting Segments

Chr	Start	End	cM
1	2514775	6589435	10.8
1	7041789	57151989	68.4
1	59833595	73262084	13.8
1	144454453	162900145	22.9
1	163857300	173563071	10.5
1	199655922	214805411	22.0
1	219905499	247179501	48.8
2	8674	15104427	32.7
2	65669811	71946160	7.8
2	142960968	153862593	8.3
2	216528599	220420289	8.0
3	2748049	44917125	60.4
4	21485092	41910182	26.8
4	58650421	68397763	6.3
4	84264939	113488806	25.4
4	161809541	168643100	7.6
4	184507901	168714276	14.4
5	53734292	67581509	10.8
5	167326588	169856275	6.0
6	1725690	4605846	8.2
6	20095950	29462788	10.2
6	30052127	37714282	6.5
6	83775222	91726062	6.5
6	136393419	157478971	28.3
7	66872687	108507075	40.0
7	149134776	158811981	25.5
8	3865517	20592998	30.4
8	23592043	29958342	9.4
8	56357254	99566847	37.3
8	135013702	139004665	7.0
9	24621812	113103267	70.2
10	3779223	11399475	16.5
10	14048451	95518432	19.0
10	130040309	135327873	14.1

Chr	Start	End	cM
11	70105511	76590284	6.5
12	2620073	10416911	19.2
12	20682158	29001936	11.5
12	70505603	88301990	12.6
13	17956717	23327097	9.9
13	32349662	96313752	60.1
13	104023640	109448627	16.1
14	22311251	77110927	64.7
14	81612236	106356482	44.9
15	29327189	77185161	60.1
15	85317851	90323310	9.5
15	93460189	96140221	9.1
16	3982450	56143736	67.4
16	69077284	76471974	7.8
16	77563991	80196410	9.2
17	26863816	30537704	7.9
17	50321402	61081459	13.5
17	72427902	78644427	19.5
18	3034	4347867	14.0
18	13536937	36032230	20.2
18	46431858	54921500	8.7
18	70016073	72395179	7.5
19	5930820	9210414	10.0
19	17437902	35265857	8.4
20	8495958	11507979	8.1
20	40814629	46622891	11.3
20	54545239	62381673	25.7
21	9849404	26740533	27.2
21	41470591	46014081	12.3
22	25823361	31301498	7.9
22	47482700	49542594	7.3
23	29965909	39590120	16.9
		Total cM:	1435.7

Figure 16-2

130

Rhoda and Pinchas are third cousins twice, once on Rhoda's grandfather's mother's Zwiebel side and once on her grandmother's mother's Kwoczka side. It is, therefore, all but certain that matches between them on the Zwiebel side would be interpreted falsely by the Lazarus tool to belong to Jute Leah Kwoczka.

I had to leave one of them out of the analysis and since Pinchas is one of only two people in Group 2, Rhoda would have to watch this one from the sidelines. In order to limit Group 1 to ten people, I also omitted one of my sisters.

I used the default threshold of 6 cM, and the resulting Lazarus kit is composed of sixty-six segments across all twenty-three chromosomes. Chromosome 11 has one segment of 6.5 cM. Most of the other chromosomes have more than one segment and all have much more matching DNA. Seven of the matching segments are more than 60 cM.

The total, however, is only 1435.7 cM; not enough for GEDmatch to accept it for batch processing. One more Kwoczka cousin would have been enough to get to 1500 cM but none is available at this time.

There is another option. I lowered the threshold from 6 cM to 5 cM that resulted in a kit of 1495.1 cM using the same people. Almost 1500 cM, but not quite. The lowest threshold that GEDmatch offers is 4 cM and that produced a kit of 1583 cM. Of course, as I discussed in Chapter Ten, these smaller segments are problematic.

The reconstruction of Hersch Pickholz

Group 1 for my great-grandfather can include Rhoda because Cousin Pinchas is not relevant for Group 2. But Herb is a problem. In his case, we have two Brauns, uncle and nephew, who married two Pikholz—aunt and niece. Herb is the son of the nephew and niece, while Elaine and Ralph are descendants of the uncle and aunt.

We cannot, therefore, include Herb in Group 1 because that would introduce significant amounts of Braun DNA that GEDmatch would falsely assume to be from the Pikholz family. So Group 1 for Hersch is the twelve descendants minus Herb and one of my sisters.

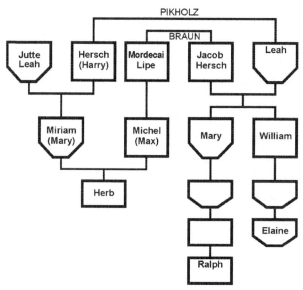

Figure 16-3

Using only the three closest cousins—Joe, Elaine, and Ralph—for Group 2 produces a very small version of Hersch's genome, 985.4 cM. That is not enough for much. I added in the descendants of Uncle Selig, Anna, and David; and the Baar-Riss cousins, Milton, Julia, and Mr. X; and barely reached the level that GEDmatch accepts for batch processing. Anna and David are related to Hersch on the side of his mother Rivka Feige (Chapter Seven) and the Baar-Riss cousins may be descended from Rivka Feige herself (Chapter Twelve).

GROUP 1	GROUP 2	Total cM	of total
10	A	985.4	13.0%
10	A B	1235.9	16.3%
10	A C	1275.4	16.9%
10	A B C	1516	20.0%
10	A B C D	1836.1	24.3%
10	A B C D E	2133.2	28.2%
10	A B C D F	2075.6	27.4%
10	A B C D E F	2343.1	31.0%

Group 1 excludes Herb and one of my sisters.

A - Joe, Elaine, Ralph
B - Anna, David (descendants of U. Selig)
C - Milton, Julia, Mr.X (Baar-Riss family)
D - Leonora, JudyT
E - Dalia, Lloyd, Barbara
F - Charles, Jane, Nan

Other descendants of
Mordecai/Taube &
Isak Josef

Figure 16-4

We must keep in mind that the choice of cousins for Group 2 should minimize the effect of endogamy. In both these groups of cousins, B and C in Figure 16-4, there is at least one non-Jewish side. That reduces the effect of endogamy from the genes of those particular cousins.

As we approach the generations of Hersch's parents and grandparents, the whole notion of being related on one side or the other becomes meaningless. In some cases, such as Leonora and JudyT, we have documentary evidence that the DNA supports. For Barbara, we surmise the connections on both sides from the DNA alone. For Anna and David, it's a combination of my father's memory, a bit of documentation, and strong DNA evidence. For the Baar-Riss cousins, it's the DNA and the naming patterns.

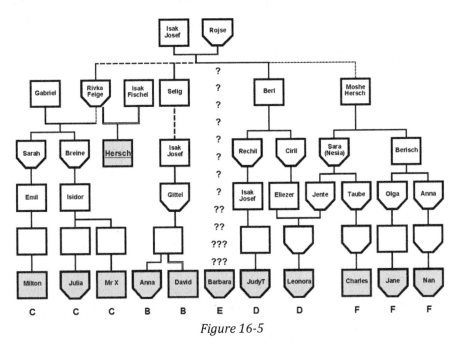

Figure 16-5

Figure 16-5 shows the members of Hersch's Group 2, as they are related to him through his mother, Rivka Feige.

Figure 16-6 shows the members of Hersch's Group 2 as they are related to Mordecai and Taube, where Mordecai is a close relative of Hersch's father Isak Fischel.

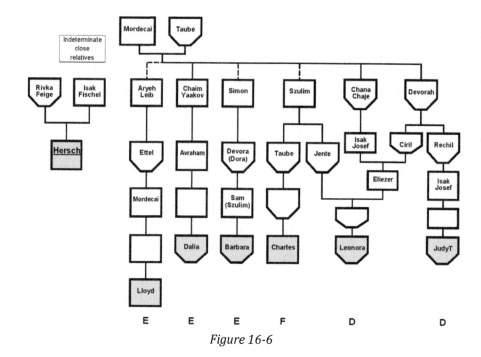

Figure 16-6

Endogamy

There are different kinds of endogamy. In this chapter, I deleted Rhoda and Herb from Group 1, and I did the same with Lee in the previous chapter. Those were because of specific known connections between these cousins and people in Group 2 outside the connection with the person being "Lazarized." Each falsely-attributed matching segment is significant, and some of them may be quite large.

The second kind of endogamy, perhaps we can call it "classic endogamy," results from our sharing of multiple distant ancestors after marrying within the tribe for hundreds of years. The matching segments from these ancestors are generally small—even very small—and affect the results only in the aggregate. Which is nothing to sneeze at.

The Group 2 cousins in my great-grandfather Hersch's Lazarus kit are something different. What we have here are multiple marriages within the family five to six generations ago. These marriages are on one hand numerous, affecting a large group of present-day descendants, yet recent enough that the descendants carry some large segments from ancestors from two or more overlapping lines. This means to my thinking that the close Pikholz endogamy

134

from the late 1700s swamps the classic endogamy from the more distant ancestors. I think, and perhaps the experts in statistical genealogy can confirm, that this turns endogamy into a benefit assisting in our analysis rather than hindering it.

For that reason, attempting to construct Lazarus kits for Hersch's parents Rivka Feige and Isak Fischel would be meaningless, even if we had the cousins we would need to do so. They would be too similar to one another.

Furthermore, in our case the DNA seems to show that the marriages within my own Pikholz family two hundred years ago were selective. The families of Isak Josef, Mordecai/Taube and Isak Fischel married each other but do not appear to have married the family of Old Nachman or the family of Peretz, even though we know from our Y-DNA matches that our family and Nachman's family have a fairly recent common male-line ancestor.

Going back to Hersch's Group 2, cousins A, B and C give us enough matching segments to meet the GEDmatch requirement of 1500 cM for batch processing which would allow comparison to the kits of outsiders. The largest component is from the A cousins, which is to be expected as they are both closer genetically (descended from Hersch's sisters) and more diverse than cousins B and C.

The D cousins, Leonora and JudyT, are both documented descendants of Berl, the son of Isak Josef, and Devorah, the daughter of Mordecai and Taube. They are clearly related to both Rivka Feige and Isak Fischel, and they add 326 cM to Hersch's Lazerus kit.

Dalia, Lloyd and Barbara, the E cousins, descend from Mordecai and Taube and contribute another 306 cM.

Finally, the F cousins, Charles, Jane, and Nan, whom I discussed in Chapter Six, match an additional 240 cM of the DNA of Group 1.

These numbers are not to be considered precise as they reflect the order in which I added them in. If, for instance, Leonora and JudyT were not already in the calculation, Dalia, Lloyd, and Barbara would surely appear to have a higher contribution.

Now that we have thirty percent of Hersch's DNA to work with, it is possible to see what kind of matches result from our possible cousins from Chapter 11. But before that, let us see how the known Pikholz descendants from Skalat who are not closely related to Hersch Pikholz match up with his Lazarus kit.

Chapter Seventeen

Cousins of Hersch

The Lazarus kit

It was time to compare the Lazarus kit of my great-grandfather Hersch Pikholz to his indeterminate relatives. These are the Pikholz descendants from Skalat who are not known to be closely related to him. I decided to use four versions of Group 2 used in creating his kit, as described in Figure 16-4. Ten of his twelve descendants make up Group 1.

The first version consists of Groups A, B, C, and D—descendants of Hersch's sisters, close relatives of his mother, and JudyT and Leonora who are clearly and closely related on both sides. This version has the smallest potential for matches but also the smallest potential for interference from endogamy.

The second version adds Group E, Dalia, Lloyd, and Barbara, known to be related on Hersch's father's side but not on his mother's side.

The third version does not include Group E but does include Group F. That would be Jane, Nan, and Charles, who are on Hersch's mother's side but not on his father's side. They are essentially as close as Group B, the descendants of Uncle Selig, but they do not feel as close. No small part of this analysis—any analysis of endogamous relationships—is undeniably subjective.

The final version includes both Groups E and F. This brings Hersch's Lazarus kit to 31 percent of his genome, but some amount of this—maybe a tenth or more—is probably not really his but is from some other relationship between someone in Group 1 (the descendants) and someone in Group 2. This is not significant on its own, but it can become significant when we look at how other people match Hersch's [partial] genome.

Matches within the family

There are five family sets that I want to compare to the Lazarus kit of Hersch Pikholz. First are the members of Groups E and F for those kits that did not use them as part of Group 2.

Third are the five descendants of Peretz Pikholz (b. ~1820). I shall be discussing this family in greater detail in Chapter Twenty.

Fourth are the seven descendants of Nachman Pikholz (1795) as they were defined in Chapter Eight.

Finally, Craig and Ron, second cousins whom we will meet in greater detail in Chapter Twenty-One.

Figure 17-1 shows how each of those twenty Pikholz descendants from Skalat matches the partially reconstructed genome of Hersch Pikholz, both by total centiMorgans and by the number of matching segments. These matches include segments of 7 cM or greater.

Matches with the Lazarus kits of Hersch Pikholz
Total cM / Number of segments (min 7 cM)

		Base group of ten 24.3%	Base group plus E 28.2%	Base group plus F 27.4%	Base group plus E&F 31.0%
Group E	Dalia	26.1 / 3	-	36.3 / 4	-
	Lloyd	11.5 / 1	-	18.7 / 2	-
	Barbara	57.9 / 4	-	59.5 / 4	-
Group F	Charles	24.2 / 2	34.1 / 3	-	-
	Jane	64.5 / 3	72.7 / 4	-	-
	Nan	43.5 / 3	44.3 / 3	-	-
Peretz Pikholz family	Irene	none	7.9 / 1	8.5 / 1	16.4 / 2
	Bruce	none	7.0 / 1	15.2 / 2	22.2 / 3
	Bonnie	10.9 / 1	18.4 / 2	24.3 / 2	31.8 / 3
	Gili	9.7 / 1	37.3 / 4	9.7 / 1	37.3 / 4
	Gene	20.8 / 2	21.1 / 2	20.8 / 2	21.1 / 2
Nachman Pikholz family	Jacob	7.2 / 1	22.2 / 3	7.2 / 1	22.2 / 3
	Filip	8.7 / 1	17.0 / 2	8.7 / 1	17.0 / 2
	Maciej	none	14.9 / 2	none	14.9 / 2
	Susan	7.2 / 1	23.2 / 3	15.1 / 2	31.0 / 4
	Rita	8.0 / 1	8.0 / 1	8.0 / 1	8.0 / 1
	Roslyn	16.0 / 2	23.4 / 3	22.2 / 2	31.2 / 3
	DavidD	23.2 / 3	49.8 / 6	44.5 / 5	63.5 / 7
Others	Craig	7.7 / 1	15.7 / 2	7.7 / 1	15.7 / 2
	Ron	8.3 / 1	29.0 / 3	17.7 / 2	38.4 / 4

The percentages are the size of Hersch's genome generated by each combination.

Figure 17-1

Keep in mind that the comparison is to a partial genome of Hersch, no greater than 31 percent. If this were a full genome, the matching segments would be perhaps three times as numerous with the number of cM increasing accordingly.

The observations that follow are just that, observations. I may think I understand what the numbers are telling me, but I may well be wrong. For now, these explanations are the best I can do.

In comparing Group E, descendants of Mordecai (1805) and Taube, to Hersch, Barbara stands out with matches approaching 60 cM. Dalia and Lloyd have smaller matches but the increase when adding Charles, Jane, and Nan (Group F) is large, while Barbara's is very small. It appears, therefore, that Dalia and Lloyd are much closer to Group F than is Barbara. Barbara has a significant Pikholz connection that we have not yet identified.

We have documented that Barbara, Dalia, and Lloyd are related to Hersch on his father's side. But while Barbara's match with Hersch is mostly on his father's side, Dalia and Lloyd seem to be related on his mother's side as well.

Moving on to Group F, the descendants of Moshe Hersch (Chapter Six), something unusual stands out. Charles, who has a double dose of Pikholz DNA, reaches a total of only 34.1 cM in common with Hersch, Nan has 44.3 cM and Jane a whopping 72.7 cM in common with Hersch. Only Nan's match does not increase significantly with the addition of Group E to Hersch's partial genome.

The difference between Charles on one hand and his third cousins Jane and Nan (second cousins to one another) can be explained by the vagaries of DNA inheritance. The difference between Jane and Nan appears truly extreme, especially when we factor in that Jane knows of no Jewish DNA from her mother.

Of the five descendants of Peretz Pikholz, four—Irene, Bonnie, Gili, and Gene—are great-grandchildren of Peretz' four daughters. Bruce is the son of Irene's first cousin. Their matches with the partial genome of Hersch do not seem to fit any pattern. Irene and Bruce do not match the base group at all, while Gene matches the base group almost exclusively. Gili matches Group E but not Group F, while Irene, Bruce, and Bonnie match Group F more than Group E.

If I were to draw one overall conclusion, it would be that the family of Peretz matches Hersch and the whole Mordecai-Taube–Isak Josef complex based more on some Original Pikholz rather than a relationship in the 1800s.

Most of Nachman's descendants show the same amorphous tendency. Maciej does not match the basic group, while Rita matches only that group.

Jacob and Filip match only the basic group and Group E. Susan and Roslyn have small matches with all three groups, but their total matches are less than 32 cM. Roslyn has a double dose of Pikholz DNA.

The one exception among Nachman's descendants is David Dekel. He has the largest match by far with each of the three groups, and his total match is 63.5 cM in seven segments. David clearly has a meaningful match—probably more than one—with my great-grandfather. A match that is not from Nachman. We saw a strong indication of that in Chapter Eight, and the partial recreation of Hersch Pikholz' genome confirms it. Tests by a few of David's first cousins would give us some guidance, but as usual, the solution lies in documentation that we do not have at this point.

There is one other thing about David Dekel. When I first met him and his sister and told him about my research project, they told me that their mother Cyla had said they are not related to the other Pikholz families in Skalat. Now that we have determined their great-grandfather Moshe Pikholz is a grandson of Old Nachman, that makes sense for none of Nachman's descendants who used the name Pikholz lived in Skalat in the 1920s when Cyla was a young woman. But now that we know from David's Family Finder test that he has a connection to the local Pikholz families that his mother did not know of, we can see that the conclusions of Chapter Eight are correct. Someone—at least one person—in David Dekel's background other than Old Nachman shares DNA with the Mordecai-Taube–Isak Josef complex.

Perhaps that connection is through David's father's families—Dligacz, Goldapper or some other—or perhaps it is through one of Cyla's female ancestors—Bomse, Willner, Muhlrad, or some other. See Figure 8-5 for that structure. It should be easy enough to determine which of those two general directions is correct. All we need is for a couple of David's first cousins to do Family Finder tests.

It is hard to draw conclusions at this point regarding the second cousins Craig and Ron. Ron's matches with my great-grandfather's partial kit are better than anyone else in the families of Peretz and Nachman aside from David Dekel. Craig's are less strong. I shall examine this family in greater depth in Chapter Twenty-One.

Having seen that it is possible to work with a Lazarus file in the 24-31 percent range and see results that make sense, we can now turn our attention to non-Pikholz matches in the same context.

Chapter Eighteen

Lessons in Endogamy

GEDmatch and the Lazarus kit

The results that GEDmatch gives for a one-to-one match are the same for a Lazarus kit as for a normal one-to-one chromosomal comparison. For each matching segment between the two kits being compared, they show the chromosome number, the starting and ending locations of the matching segment, and the size of the segment in centiMorgans (cMs) and in SNPs. I have not discussed SNPs here.

In addition, they give you the total cM for the match and the "Estimated number of generations to MRCA" (most recent common ancestor). All this is based on the threshold you set to exclude small segments. Their default is 7 cM, and I have not changed that. If you want to know how many matching segments a pair of kits has, you can count them yourself.

I have no idea how GEDmatch calculates the number of generations to the MRCA, but I assume they know what they are doing. Obviously, their algorithm takes into account the number of matching segments and their sizes and the size of the largest and the total of all the matches. As far as I know, they do not take into account the endogamy factor—as does Family Tree DNA in their suggested relationships—although they have a tool called "Are your parents related" they could probably factor in if they wanted to.

In comparing the eighteen non-Pikholz from Chapter Eleven to the partial Lazarus kit of my great-grandfather Hersch Pikholz, I decided that there is no reason not to use the largest Lazarus kit that consists of 31 percent of his genome. For the matches from before Original Skalat Pikholz, who was probably born around the 1750s, I see no reason to differentiate within the various groups that I cited in Chapter Seventeen.

Figure 18-1 shows how each of the eighteen non-Pikholz matches the Lazarus kit of Hersch Pikholz. The column with the predicted number of generations to a common ancestor—and remember, Hersch was born in the early 1850s—is color-coded.

Ruth, my second cousin on my mother's side, is a special case and appears far closer than everyone else. On one hand, I would like to say that this has to do with her other connections with my family not connected to Hersch. On the other hand, the Lazarus process should have weeded out these irrelevant matches. We don't know the details of Ruth's father's lineage, but unless he is a very close relative of the Pikholz clan from the 1800s, there is no way Ruth should appear so close to Hersch. The lesson here is that no matter how hard you try or how deliberate your efforts are, there are endogamous elements to all these European Jewish relationships. You can only hope to contain them.

Matches with the partial (31%) Lazarus kit
of Hersch Pikholz (min 7 cM)
Does not include X-chromosome

	Total cM	Number of segments	Largest segment	Predicted generations
JoAnne	41.8	5	9.6	4.6
Mark	30.8	4	8.3	6.2
JudiZ	7.7	1	7.7	**7.4**
SarahC	23.8	3	8.4	6.2
Victor	27.2	3	10.5	4.5
Cynthia	23.3	3	8.4	6.2
Alexandra	33.2	4	9.2	5.2
David Ari	12.3	1	12.3	5.1
Lily	20.1	2	10.4	4.7
Lily's mom	17.4	2	9.6	5.2
SteveT	25.5	3	9.2	5.3
Steve's mom	14.7	2	7.4	**7.0**
MarlaW	37.0	4	10.6	4.3
Marla's mom	24.8	3	9.8	4.8
SharonG	31.7	4	9.2	5.2
GaryG	15.7	2	8.5	6.5
Ruth	76.6	9	10.5	3.8
D. Goldin	8.7	1	8.7	6.7

Figure 18-1

I am not even sure that using Kitty Cooper's mapping tool, which I touched upon briefly in Chapter Fifteen, it would be possible to improve on results such as Ruth's here. We are one people, and we are one family; the answers are not in genetics but in traditional genealogy methods.

Relatives

One might expect that since Victor and Cynthia are second cousins—that is, they have common great-grandparents who probably lived about the same time as Hersch, their matches with Hersch might be similar. As we see in Figure 18-2, one would be wrong.

Not only are they completely different, but Victor appears more than a generation and a half closer to Hersch than Cynthia.

Victor's match

Chr	Start Location	End Location	cM	SNPs
2	11,839,505	18,005,614	10.5	1588
3	24,733,372	30,806,154	7.8	1707
18	68,665,099	71,278,968	8.9	1016

Largest segment = 10.5 cM
Total of segments > 7 cM = 27.2 cM
Estimated number of generations to MRCA = 4.5

Cynthia's's match

Chr	Start Location	End Location	cM	SNPs
2	112,164,359	121,043,984	7.5	1879
20	5,781,688	8,717,423	7.5	1001
22	19,753,933	23,564,481	8.4	738

Largest segment = 8.4 cM
Total of segments > 7 cM = 23.3 cM
Estimated number of generations to MRCA = 6.2

Figure 18-2

David Ari and Pamela (Lily's mom) are also second cousins. They are about the same distance generationally from Hersch, but they too match on different segments.

Lily

Chr	Start Location	End Location	cM	SNPs
9	116003697	123416410	9.7	2052
14	57503986	70209032	10.4	2978

Largest segment = 10.4 cM
Total of segments > 7 cM = 20.1 cM
Estimated number of generations to MRCA = 4.7

Lily's mom

Chr	Start Location	End Location	cM	SNPs
2	111720338	121005862	7.8	1914
9	116011205	123384259	9.6	2036

Largest segment = 9.6 cM
Total of segments > 7 cM = 17.4 cM
Estimated number of generations to MRCA = 5.2

Steve

Chr	Start Location	End Location	cM	SNPs
4	176991669	18175796	7.4	1291
6	41721750	45864457	8.8	1083
22	25519536	31255170	9.2	1608

Largest segment = 9.2 cM
Total of segments > 7 cM = 25.5 cM
Estimated number of generations to MRCA = 5.3

Steve's mom

Chr	Start Location	End Location	cM	SNPs
7	4128319	7920431	7.4	1015
21	41508474	43437235	7.4	964

Largest segment = 9.2 cM
Total of segments > 7 cM = 25.5 cM
Estimated number of generations to MRCA = 5.3

Marla

Chr	Start Location	End Location	cM	SNPs
1	10880571	14025036	7.1	706
1	14090261	18515834	10.6	1379
19	56265850	58801619	9.5	892
22	43173024	46773410	9.8	1307

Largest segment = 10.6 cM
Total of segments > 7 cM = 37.0 cM
Estimated number of generations to MRCA = 4.3

Marla's mom

Chr	Start Location	End Location	cM	SNPs
1	10880571	14036072	7.1	712
1	14456059	18578281	9.8	1237
14	98409650	101006560	7.9	797

Largest segment = 9.8 cM
Total of segments > 7 cM = 24.8 cM
Estimated number of generations to MRCA = 4.9

Figure 18-3

In Figure 18-3, we can compare Lily, Steve, and Marla's matches to their mothers' matches. In all three cases, as we saw in Chapter Eleven, the children have matches from their fathers' sides so they are closer to the Pikholz families than their mothers are. In the cases of Lily and Marla, the difference is half a generation or less, while Steve is 1.7 generations closer than his mother indicating a very significant contribution from his father. That's even more when you consider that Steve is one generation younger than his mother, so there are really 2.7 generations from his father.

Lily and Pamela have almost identical matches on chromosome 9. Lily did not inherit Pamela's match on chromosome 2, but she received a match on chromosome 14 from her father.

Steve received neither of his mother's matching segments, but has three that came from his father.

Marla received both her mother's matches from chromosome 1, but not the one on chromosome 14. Marla's father gave her two matching Pikholz segments.

This is endogamy and anyone who would try to draw conclusions without taking that into account will surely err. This is another reason to test everyone you can—you never know what might turn up.

The unknowns

The genome that is my great-grandfather's Lazarus kit is not a full genome. It represents only 31 percent of his DNA. Does this mean that the 33.2 cM that Alexandra shares with him and the 31.7 cM that Sharon shares with him are really more like 100 cM? Maybe, but these things are statistical so maybe it's significantly more and maybe it's significantly less.

Does that mean that Sharon and Alexandra are much closer to Hersch than 5.2 generations? Or maybe they are like Steve, and they only appear to be that close because they share DNA with Hersch from their mothers and their fathers. Or for that matter, maybe what Marla and Lily have from their mothers is actually part from the grandmothers and part from the grandfathers. The endogamous nature of European Jewry says that is probably the case. We all come from that same set of ancestors who lived in Europe five hundred years ago, plus those refugees from Spain who came into the Ashkenazic gene pool in the decades that followed.

For that matter, Hersch himself is the son of two Pikholz descendants, probably no further than second cousins. And I would be surprised if one or both sets of his grandparents were not cousins as well. That, of course, makes Hersch look closer to his matches than he actually is. How much closer? It depends on any number of things.

JoAnne's matching segments total 41.8 cM, and GEDmatch tells us that the most recent common ancestor she shares with Hersch is a distance of 4.6 generations. That's what GEDmatch does with the numbers it sees. But those 41.8 cM are on five segments.

JoAnne's matching segments

Chr	Start Location	End Location	cM	SNPs
13	110126564	113281796	7.9	912
14	97755176	100858600	9.2	981
18	69690285	71869625	7.0	785
19	4591983	7405624	8.1	767
20	5475176	8957406	9.6	1137

Largest segment = 9.6 cM
Total of segments > 7 cM = 41.8 cM
Estimated number of generations to MRCA = 4.6

Figure 18-4

Those five segments are between 7 and 9.6 cM. Perhaps each one represents a different pathway to a common ancestor with Hersch, each of those ancestors seven generations back in time. We cannot know this with DNA. We can only know this using traditional genealogy tools and methods.

There is something magic about DNA. It can give you a clear picture about close relationships and about distant relationships on the all-male and all-female line. It can also help you jump to false conclusions if that's what you have a mind to do.

We *do* know that it cannot do everything.

But there may be one other thing this Lazarus test can do.

Rozdol and Skalat—one family or two, redux

As I said in the introduction, before we entered the world of genetic genealogy I was reconciled to the idea that the Pikholz families from Skalat and

Rozdol were probably two families rather than one. In fact, my plans for a genetic study of the Pikholz families was planned only for the Skalat descendants.

In Chapter Four, when Gary forced my hand and we had our first Rozdol tests, I began to see that there were quite a few matches between members of the two families. From that point on, I decided that they were probably a single family that had drifted apart some two hundred years ago.

But in the course of things, I began to have doubts even though I never spoke or wrote of them. There were so many non-Pikholz who matched so many of us that I began to wonder if the Rozdol-Skalat matches were not the normal results of garden-variety endogamy. I was not sure how to test that.

Figure 18-5 shows how the twelve Rozdolers match my great-grandfather's Lazarus kit.

Matches with the partial (31%) Lazarus kit
of Hersch Pikholz (min 7 cM)
Does not include X-chromosome

	Total cM	Number of segments	Largest segment	Predicted generations
Gary	18.2	2	9.6	5.2
Esther	19.3	2	11.9	4.8
Micha	45.2	4	19.0	4.2
Francis	49.5	6	9.3	4.8
Miriam	22.4	3	7.8	6.7
Pawel	16.0	2	8.4	6.5
Amos	14.4	2	7.3	7.0
Ira	22.5	3	7.7	6.7
Steve	20.0	2	10.3	4.7
Robert	25.7	3	9.9	4.6
Rosa	25.0	3	9.2	5.3
Marion	49.8	6	8.8	5.3

Figure 18-5

Let's recount. Gary and Esther are cousins. Micha, Francis, and Miriam are cousins. Pawel and Amos are cousins. Ira and Steve are cousins. Robert, Rosa, and Marion are cousins.

Some of these matches with Hersch Pikholz are quite good. Others, not so much. Pawel and Amos are quite distant. The second cousins Ira and Steve are contradictory, with Steve as a good match and Ira a very weak match. Miriam is a much weaker match than her cousins Micha and Francis.

Gary and Esther look good, as do Robert, Rosa, and Marion. But it is not convincing. Is this whole set that much better matched to Hersch Pikholz than the set of non-Pikholz who are surely from the early or mid-1700s at best?

Perhaps the matching segments can tell us something. The thirty-eight matching segments are spread across fifteen of the twenty-two chromosomes. Chromosomes 5, 9, 10, 12. 13, 16, and 21 have no matches between Hersch Pikholz and the Rozdolers. Chromosomes 3, 8, 15, 17, and 19 have one match each. Three of them are with Francis. On chromosomes 1, 6, 7, 20 and 22 we have two matches but only on chromosome 7 do the two come on the same segment. That would be Miriam and Robert.

We have three matches on two chromosomes. On chromosome 2, Ira and Rosa are on the same segment, and Robert does not match them. On chromosome 11, Micha and Amos are on the same segment, and Ira does not match them.

Chromosome 4 has four matches. Gary, Francis, and Robert are all on the same segment with Steve elsewhere on the chromosome.

Chromosome 18 has five matches; two of them are Marion. On one, Marion matches Francis. On the other, she matches Micha and Miriam.

That leaves chromosome 14, where we have eight matches. Here too, Marion is represented twice. On one, she matches Francis and Ira. On the other, she matches no one. The other four—Esther, Micha, Pawel, and Rosa all match each other. These four are from different parts of the Rozdol Pikholz family.

Out of twelve Rozdol testers, we have one matching set of four, three sets of three, and four sets of two. On the basis of the matching segments, I am back to saying that the Pikholz families from Skalat and Rozdol are one.

Figure 18-6 on the next page depicts these matches.

146

Rosa

Chr	Start Location	End Location	Centimorgans (cM)
1	166575771	175650659	8.1
2	13006677	17873374	7.6
14	96973226	100379512	9.2

Largest segment = 9.2 cM
Total of segments > 7 cM = 25.0 cM
Estimated # of generations to MRCA = 5.3

Ira

Chr	Start Location	End Location	Centimorgans (cM)
2	12840374	17155408	7.3
11	46225065	65577249	7.4
14	21857381	25461047	7.7

Largest segment = 7.7 cM
Total of segments > 7 cM = 22.5 cM
Estimated # of generations to MRCA = 6.7

Robert

Chr	Start Location	End Location	Centimorgans (cM)
2	96789288	107182845	7.1
4	803393	6083702	9.9
7	3237421	7808049	8.7

Largest segment = 9.9 cM
Total of segments > 7 cM = 25.7 cM
Estimated # of generations to MRCA = 4.6

Miriam

Chr	Start Location	End Location	Centimorgans (cM)
1	242646142	245196568	7.4
7	4016802	7807948	7.3
18	57321787	61615240	7.8

Largest segment = 7.8 cM
Total of segments > 7 cM = 22.4 cM
Estimated # of generations to MRCA = 6.7

Micha

Chr	Start Location	End Location	Centimorgans (cM)
11	59581102	78380174	19.0
14	98504041	100972552	7.6
18	56003567	61865109	10.2
22	32601782	35954182	8.4

Largest segment = 19.0 cM
Total of segments > 7 cM = 45.2 cM
Estimated # of generations to MRCA = 4.2

Esther

Chr	Start Location	End Location	Centimorgans (cM)
14	96802345	100874929	11.9
20	5599216	8281770	7.4

Largest segment = 11.9 cM
Total of segments > 7 cM = 19.3 cM
Estimated # of generations to MRCA = 4.8

Francis

Chr	Start Location	End Location	Centimorgans (cM)
4	61566	5520119	8.7
8	135010026	139494059	8.3
14	22665263	27466854	9.3
17	71265098	74041888	8.2
18	69591642	71715844	7.0
19	60394722	63774647	8.0

Largest segment = 9.3 cM
Total of segments > 7 cM = 49.5 cM
Estimated # of generations to MRCA = 4.8

Steve

Chr	Start Location	End Location	Centimorgans (cM)
3	24698932	31955610	9.7
4	35036847	41772998	10.3

Largest segment = 10.3 cM
Total of segments > 7 cM = 20.0 cM
Estimated # of generations to MRCA = 4.7

Pawel

Chr	Start Location	End Location	Centimorgans (cM)
6	41751223	45628550	8.4
14	98465407	100938782	7.6

Largest segment = 8.4 cM
Total of segments > 7 cM = 16.0 cM
Estimated # of generations to MRCA = 6.5

Marion

Chr	Start Location	End Location	Centimorgans (cM)
6	1050037318	112043271	8.7
14	22444702	25772675	7.6
14	61465721	71092644	8.5
18	56945896	62138659	8.8
18	69605732	72139127	8.2
20	7147413	10112632	8.1

Largest segment = 8.8 cM
Total of segments > 7 cM = 49.8 cM
Estimated # of generations to MRCA = 5.3

Gary

Chr	Start Location	End Location	Centimorgans (cM)
4	61566	5803954	9.6
22	26001082	32400821	8.5

Largest segment = 9.6 cM
Total of segments > 7 cM = 18.2 cM
Estimated # of generations to MRCA = 5.2

Amos

Chr	Start Location	End Location	Centimorgans (cM)
11	65393849	71959532	7.3
15	93458392	95574980	7.0

Largest segment = 7.3 cM
Total of segments > 7 cM = 14.4 cM
Estimated # of generations to MRCA = 7.0

Figure 18-6

147

Chapter Nineteen

Imperfect Triangulation
Amos and Pawel, Ira and Steve

Amos and Pawel

The big sale by Family Tree DNA in December 2014 which played a large role in my being able to write this book saw twenty-three new Family Finder tests for my family projects, in addition to several Y-DNA and MtDNA tests and a few upgrades. Other than the Y-37 upgrade to Micha's test that I discussed in Chapter Four, the only Rozdol Pikholz test was a Family Finder by Pawel. Several others expressed an interest and even accepted discount coupons, but only Pawel followed through. Pawel's father is a first cousin of Amos whom I also introduced in Chapter Four.

The original Rozdol couple, Sara Rivka and Pinchas, has documented sons Israel Yoel and Aron. They appear to have sons Berl (about whom we know nothing), Samuel (or more likely David Samuel), and the Isak-Feige group that I discussed in Chapter Four, which has at least six children. There are four other families with living descendants that we can trace back to grandchildren or great-grandchildren of the founding couple, but we cannot bridge the generational gap from those four to Pinchas and Sara Rivka.

The four families are headed by Pinchas (~1830s), Gittel (~1830s), Isak (~1850s), and Pinchas (~1860s). Gittel stands out as being the only Pikholz family in Rozdol that traces back to a woman, and she is the great-great-grandmother of Pawel and the great-grandmother of Amos.

Of the other ten Rozdol Pikholz descendants who did Family Finder tests aside from Amos and Pawel, two (Micha and Esther) are in the same generation as Amos; seven are in the same generation as Pawel; and one, Marion, is in the generation following Pawel. To complicate it further, Gary and Esther are each descended from two different Pikholz ancestors from the generation of Amos and Pawel's Gittel. The probability of identifying meaningful DNA matches from that long ago is extremely low.

THE ROZDOL PIKHOLZ FAMILIES

People whose names are shaded have done DNA tests

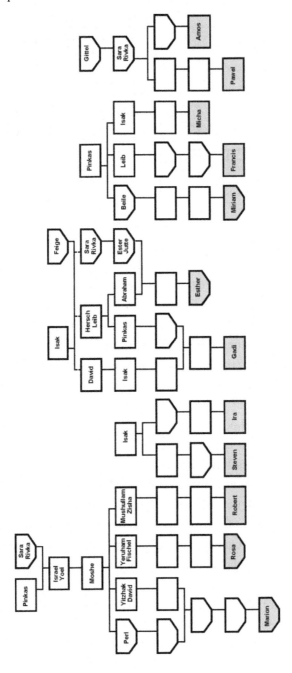

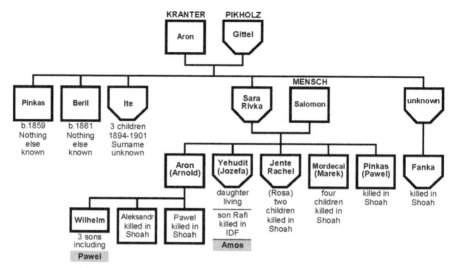

Figure 19-1

The eight in Pawel's generation are four generations removed from their ancestors born in the 1820s and 1830s, whom we would like to identify as grandchildren of the original Rozdol couple. When I discussed the family of Moshe Hersch in Chapter Six, the tests for his descendants were done by people only three generations removed from the putative siblings. And when I examined the descendants of Uncle Selig in Chapter Seven the distance was four generations from the siblings, but we had the advantage of looking at many descendants of Rivka Feige including representatives of three of her children. In the case of Amos and Pawel we are working with fewer samples by far, which reduces the chances of finding anything significant.

But nonetheless, it was worth a try.

I created a chromosome browser for Amos using GEDmatch, comparing him to Pawel and the other ten Rozdol descendants. I created a second chromosome browser for Pawel the same way and examined the two together. I wanted to see who from Rozdol matched Amos and Pawel together on segments of at least 5 cM and who matched one, but not the other, on segments of at least 10 cM.

A summary of the results, in figure 19-2, supports what was probably the most likely scenario—that the parents of Gittel, the ancestor of Amos and Pawel, were probably Isak and Feige. The size of the matches in cM is in parentheses.

Chr.	Matches with Amos	Matches with Pawel	Matches with both
2		Rosa (24)	
4	Rosa (12)	Gary (12), Marion (10)	
5		Rosa (11)	
6	Gary (16) Esther (32) & Gary (9)		
7	see Figure 19-3		Gary & Esther
9			Esther (6.8-8)
10			Robert (6-6.8)
12	Esther (18)		
14	Esther (25)		
16	Gary matches both for 7.3 cM, then continues with Amos for 12 more		
17			Robert (8.6)
18		Miriam (10.7) & Francis (6.9)	
21			Robert (6.5-7.1)
22		Miriam (15) & Micha (8)	

Figure 19-2

Esther and Gary are both descendants of Isak and Feige in two lines, one of which they share. Amos has a large match with Gary on chromosome 6, and on that same chromosome, he has a very large match with Esther that is partly shared with Gary. On chromosomes 12 and 14, Amos has large matches with Esther alone.

Pawel has a match with Gary on chromosome 4, but none with Esther that he does not share with Amos. Pawel also has a match with Miriam and Francis together on chromosome 18 and with Miriam and Micha together on chromosome 22. Miriam, Francis, and Micha are descendants of the Pinchas who I believe to be the son of Isak and Feige born in 1832.

Amos also has a match with Rosa, and Pawel has two matches with Rosa and one with Marion. Rosa and Marion are documented descendants of the original couple Pinchas and Sara Rivka.

Moving to the third column that lists matches with Amos and Pawel on the same segments, there are smallish matches with Esther (chromosome 9) and Robert (chromosomes 10, 17 and 21). Robert is also a documented descendant of the original Pinchas and Sara Rivka.

On chromosome 7 (see Figure 19-3), Amos and Pawel match each other on only 8.3 cM, but both Esther and Gary match both of them on that segment and then some. They match Pawel before his match with Amos, and they match Amos after his match with Pawel.

Amos' matches

Name	Matching segments on Chromosome 7
Esther	140018 - 7152277 (11.2061 cM), 107243556 - 111175708 (3.321 cM)
Gary	2280133 - 7152277 (8.67477 cM), 141775963 - 146554794 (5.37799 cM)
Pawel	2519512 - 7161284 (8.33282 cM), 130918978 - 133829855 (3.797 cM)

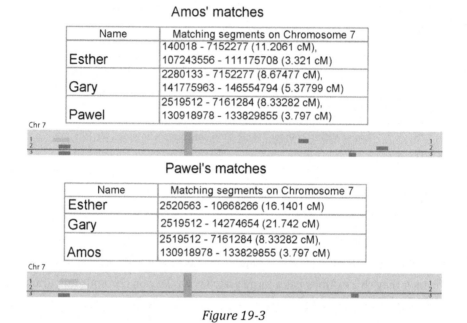

Pawel's matches

Name	Matching segments on Chromosome 7
Esther	2520563 - 10668266 (16.1401 cM)
Gary	2519512 - 14274654 (21.742 cM)
Amos	2519512 - 7161284 (8.33282 cM), 130918978 - 133829855 (3.797 cM)

Figure 19-3

On chromosome 16 (Figure 19-4), both Amos and Pawel match Gary, but Amos's matching segment is much longer than Pawel's.

Figure 19-4

It appears, therefore, that Amos and Pawel are part of the same section of the family as Esther and Gary, who are double descendants of Isak and Feige. The connection with the main-line descendants Robert, Marion, and Rosa is weaker, as is the connection to Miriam-Micha-Francis. There seems to be next to nothing between Amos and Pawel on one hand and the second cousins Ira and Steve on the other. In fact, Ira and Pawel do not match on GEDmatch at all, nor do Amos and Steve.

But of course recording Amos and Pawel's ancestor Gittel as the daughter of Isak and Feige requires documentation. Absent that, tests by additional descendants of Isak and Feige would be useful, as well as tests by the unrepresented parts of the Rozdol family.

Ira and Steve

Ira and Steve are great-grandsons of Isak Pikholz and his wife Toby Blum. This is one of our two "short" trees from Rozdol—enough generations to be considered a tree (in this case, six), but not going back to the 1830s. Isak and Toby had five known children, but only three were known to have survived childhood. All three went to the United States. The older two, Steve's grandfather and Ira's grandmother, were born in the early 1880s so Isak was probably born in the late 1850s. That would likely place him as a child of someone born in the 1820s or 1830s.

Isak died in the early 1920s, so ten years from now we may find a Polish death record that names his father. More likely one without his parents' names since his children were abroad.

I prepared the same type of chromosome browser summary that I used for Amos and Pawel—matches of more than 5 cM with both Ira and Steve, and matches of more than 10 cM with either Ira or Steve.

Here too, Gary and Esther have the most significant matches, but the other two groups are also represented. There are matches between the groups that were not present for Amos and Pawel. Steve has a match on chromosome 15 with Marion and Francis, and Ira has a large match on chromosome 16 with Gary, Esther, and Rosa.

But it would be irresponsible to draw any conclusions from the DNA—certainly without additional testing.

There is also the problem here with Isak as head of the family. As we saw in Chapter Four, it appears there are two contemporaneous Isak Pikholz, perhaps brothers-in-law—one certainly alive in 1879 and one almost certainly dead in the early or mid-1850s.

Chr.	Matches with Steve	Matches with Ira	Matches with both
1		Gary (26), Francis (11), Esther (13)	
3	Gary (16)		
4		Esther (15 & 19)	
5		Miriam (10), Francis (11)	
7	Francis (10)	Esther (16)	Esther (13)
8	Robert (18)		
9		Gary (27), Micha (17)	
10			Micha (9.5)
12	Robert (10.5)		
15	Esther (12), Marion (17) & Francis (15)		
16		Gary, Esther & Rosa (19), Gary (29) & Amos (11.5)	
22	Esther (15), Gary (10), Marion (10.5)		

Figure 19-5

Gary's great-grandfather Isak was born in the 1850s so he would be a grandson of the Isak who had died by then, as would Ira and Steve's Isak. Esther's grandmother's family would fit in that group as well. The line that Gary and Esther share could be from the long-lived Isak, as I know of no Isak there until about 1885. The family of Francis-Micha-Miriam could also be from the long-lived Isak, as the first one in that family was Micha's grandfather who was born in 1881.

Imperfect Triangulation

There is, however, one other issue that comes up in the analysis of these pairs of cousins. Let us look at Ira and Steve's matches with Esther on chromosome 7.

The long bar on the top of each set of matches represents a match between Steve and Ira of over 66 cM. The short bars underneath the long bars are Esther's matches with each of them. This looks like normal triangulation. Ira and Steve match, Esther and Steve match, and Esther and Ira match—all in a way that appears perfectly normal. There appears to be no possibility that Esther just happens to match both Steve and Ira in the same place on their non-Pikholz side.

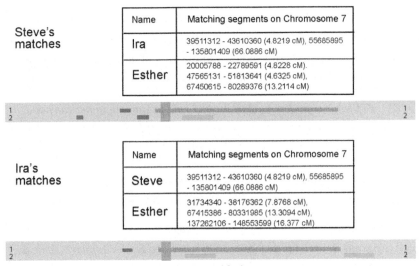

	Name	Matching segments on Chromosome 7
Steve's matches	Ira	39511312 - 43610360 (4.8219 cM), 55685895 - 135801409 (66.0886 cM)
	Esther	20005788 - 22789591 (4.8228 cM). 47565131 - 51813641 (4.6325 cM), 67450615 - 80289376 (13.2114 cM)

	Name	Matching segments on Chromosome 7
Ira's matches	Steve	39511312 - 43610360 (4.8219 cM), 55685895 - 135801409 (66.0886 cM)
	Esther	31734340 - 38176362 (7.8768 cM), 67415386 - 80331985 (13.3094 cM), 137262106 - 148553599 (16.377 cM)

Figure 19-6

However, if you look closely at the numbers Esther's match with Steve is 13.2114 cM while her match with Ira is 13.3094 cM. Does that matter? Let's consider an analogy. If Ira and Steve sit down to dinner for sixty-six consecutive minutes and Esther joins them for thirteen minutes, there is no logical way she could have sat with one even one second more than with the other. So what is going on here—did the three of them sit at the same table or not?

When I first encountered this problem, I decided to see how this chromosome looked on the FTDNA browser. (Figure 19-7)

Steve's matches

	Start	End	cM
Ira	40,122,149	43,468,742	3.54
Ira	55,849,693	135,529,672	65.30
Esther	20,055,513	22,679,402	4.43
Esther	47,762,189	51,792,039	3.35
Esther	67,711,326	80,123,786	13.04

Ira's matches

	Start	End	cM
Steve	40,122,149	43,468,742	3.54
Steve	55,849,693	135,529,672	65.30
Esther	31,796,620	38,124,406	7.54
Esther	67,711,326	80,123,786	13.04
Esther	137,575,959	148,260,692	14.84

Figure 19-7

The numbers here are slightly different because FTDNA and GEDmatch measure slightly differently. The long match between Steve and Ira is 66 cM according to GEDmatch but only 65.3 cM according to FTDNA.

But on FTDNA, Esther's match is 13.04 cM with both Steve and Ira—a perfect triangulation. Perhaps this is just an error on the part of GEDmatch. That's what I thought when I blogged about this phenomenon back in March 2015. In the ensuing discussion on Facebook, Ann Turner pointed out that:

> "FTDNA is engaged in an unusual form of rounding under the hood. It rounds segments to the nearest block of 100 SNPs, which is why so many segments *appear* to start and/or end at exactly the same base."

Regarding the original problem that I saw with GEDmatch, that Esther's matches with Ira and Steve were not identical, Ann wrote:

> "That would be an example of "fuzzy boundaries." Esther's other parent contributed a few SNPs that made it *appear* that the segment was longer in one case. The shorter segment would be closer to the true boundary, but it can still be fuzzy."

This is apparently the case. I went back to the matches that Amos and Pawel have with Robert (Figure 19-2). This is similar to the phenomenon I mentioned in Chapter Ten and which Roberta Estes calls "Identical by Chance," only here it is attached to a legitimate segment.

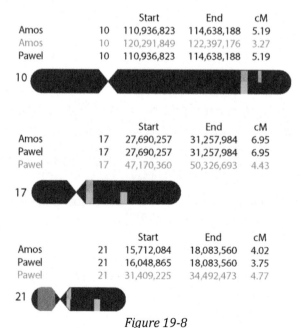

		Start	End	cM
Amos	10	110,936,823	114,638,188	5.19
Amos	10	120,291,849	122,397,176	3.27
Pawel	10	110,936,823	114,638,188	5.19

		Start	End	cM
Amos	17	27,690,257	31,257,984	6.95
Pawel	17	27,690,257	31,257,984	6.95
Pawel	17	47,170,360	50,326,693	4.43

		Start	End	cM
Amos	21	15,712,084	18,083,560	4.02
Pawel	21	16,048,865	18,083,560	3.75
Pawel	21	31,409,225	34,492,473	4.77

Figure 19-8

These are the three matches on the FTDNA chromosome browser showing how Amos (on the top) and Pawel (on the bottom) match Robert.

Robert's matches with Amos and Pawel on chromosomes 10 and 17 are congruent, while on chromosome 21 they are similar but not congruent.

On GEDmatch (Figure 19-9, following page), Robert 's match with Pawel is 8.615 cM and with Amos is 8.618 cM on chromosome 17—not quite identical in length, and the start and end points do not line up perfectly.

On chromosomes 10 and 21, the matching segments are more clearly not identical. So my analogy about sharing the table does not hold, and Ann Turner's point is conceded.

Unfortunately, only twelve Rozdolers have tested thus far, so we are limited in what we can do. I would like to think this will change, perhaps because of this book.

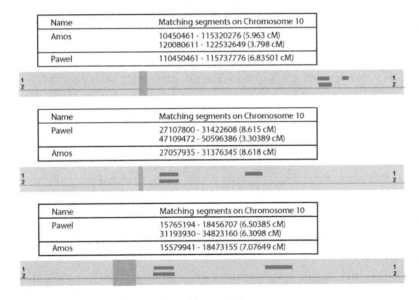

Name	Matching segments on Chromosome 10
Amos	10450461 - 115320276 (5.963 cM) 120080611 - 122532649 (3.798 cM)
Pawel	110450461 - 115737776 (6.83501 cM)

Name	Matching segments on Chromosome 10
Pawel	27107800 - 31422608 (8.615 cM) 47109472 - 50596386 (3.30389 cM)
Amos	27057935 - 31376345 (8.618 cM)

Name	Matching segments on Chromosome 10
Pawel	15765194 - 18456707 (6.50385 cM) 31193930 - 34823160 (6.3098 cM)
Amos	15579941 - 18473155 (7.07649 cM)

Figure 19-9

Chapter Twenty

Peretz

The known family of Peretz Pikholz

Among the earliest people in Skalat with the surname Pikholz are Isak Josef (1784-1862), Nachman (1795-1865), and Mordecai (1805-1864) and his wife Taube (1802-1872). Their descendants have made numerous appearances in previous chapters. The birth years are derived from their death records, so they may not be precise. There are three others about whom we know nothing at all, other than what is on their death records: Riwe (1843, age 70), Beile (1841, age 60—called "alien"), and Leib (1844, age 64).

There is one other known Pikholz born before 1810—Berl who died in 1877 at age eighty-eight. Berl and his wife Feige had two known children, Moses (b. 1823) and Sara Bassie (died 1884 at age 47). Considering the age difference between Moses and Sara Bassie, there may have been additional children.

Moses had four sons, and Sara Bassie had a son and a daughter. Each had a son with the middle name Peryc (=Peretz) born 1874 and 1875. For this reason, I believe that Peretz Pikholz, who died in 1873 at age fifty-three, is the son of this same Berl. I have doubts about Feige's being Peretz' mother, as Berl's wife seems to have been born in 1805, but that is neither here nor there for now.

We know nothing about the children of Moses and Sara Bassie beyond their birth records.

Peretz Pikholz and his wife Perl Nagler had five documented children—four daughters and a son. Peretz' son Yaakov had nine children, three of whom were known to have left Europe, but none has a male-line descendant. So we have no candidate for a Y-DNA test. His female descendants have thus far declined to do Family Finder tests. We do, however, have one great-grandchild of each of Peretz' four daughters. These four third cousins were joined by Bruce, the first cousin once removed of Irene.

158

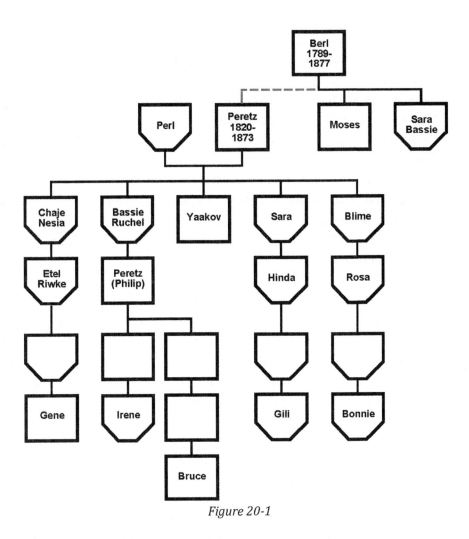

Figure 20-1

The twenty-two chromosomes

In Chapter Nineteen, I compared the GEDmatch chromosome browsers for Pawel and Amos, and later for Ira and Steve, in charts. Here it is more complex because we have five people who tested, so that will not work. Let me go through chromosome by chromosome, looking for other Skalat Pikholz descendants who match several of the descendants of Peretz on the same segments or whose matches are at least 10 cM. The sizes of the matches in cM are in parentheses. Matches are independent unless indicated otherwise.

Chromosome 1: Irene has a match with Dalia (17). Bonnie has matches with Elaine (10.8) and Craig (10.2). Gili matches Dalia (14.5). Gene matches Anna (11), Barbara (10.5), and Nan (11.6).

Chromosome 2: Bruce matches Rhoda (12). Irene matches DavidD (13.5 & 12) and Julia (10.3). Gene matches Roslyn (12.9). Gili matches Barbara, Aunt Betty, Uncle Bob, and three of my sisters all in the same segment (10-11.5). Gili's matches triangulate.

Chromosome 3: Bonnie matches Ralph (19.8). She also matches JudyT, Terry, Herb, and two of my sisters (~11) on partially congruent segments. Gili matches Aunt Betty and Uncle Bob on congruent segments (12.3). She also matches Uncle Selig's David (14.3) as well as Leonora and six of my close family on nearly congruent segments (~10). Gene matches Leonora (19).

Chromosome 4: Irene matches Barbara (12.5) on a segment that Irene matches Bruce. However, Barbara does not match Bruce there, so this is likely an endogamous match on Irene's mother's side. Bonnie matches Ralph (15.4). Gili matches Marty (12.8) and Barbara (10.9) on the same segment, with successful triangulation. Gene matches Dalia (10.7).

Chromosome 5: Bruce matches Vladimir (10) on a segment where he overlaps with Irene and Bonnie. Vladimir does not match them on that segment. Bruce matches Lloyd, Aunt Betty, and Uncle Bob on nearly congruent segments (~10), however, they do not triangulate. Irene matches Leonora (16.8). Bonnie matches Rhoda (11). Gili matches Aunt Betty (10.5). Gene matches Vladimir (11.2). Gene also matches Anna and David, Uncle Bob, and two of my sisters on nearly congruent segments (7-8).

Chromosome 6: Bruce matches DavidD (10.2). He also has two smaller matches with Craig that should match Irene, but only one of them does. On the other hand, Irene has two small matches with Barbara that should match Bruce, but they don't. Irene matches JudyT (11.1). Gene matches Leonora (18.2).

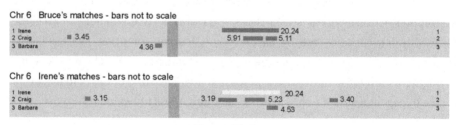

Figure 20-2

Chromosome 7: Bruce and Gili match Ron on the same segment (10.7 & 6). Bonnie matches Dalia (10.2). Bonnie also matches Marty, two of my sisters, and me on segments that all start at the same place (~10). She matches Irene on an overlapping segment, but Irene does not match the rest of us there. Gene matches Leonora twice (13.9 & 10.5) and Uncle Bob (12.7).

Does anyone else see what I am seeing? Lots of matches with descendants of Isak Josef and Mordecai, but nothing with descendants of Nachman. It makes me think that Peretz' putative father Berl is the brother of Isak Josef and perhaps the father of Mordecai and Isak Fischel. The non-matches with Nachman's descendants make me think that Nachman is a cousin of Isak Josef and Berl, rather than a brother. But I am getting ahead of myself.

Chromosome 8: Bruce matches Charles (17.9) and JudyT (14.9) on overlapping segments, but they do not triangulate. Bruce also matches Julia and Mr. X on nearly congruent segments (~10.9). Irene matches Barbara (12.5). Gili matches Ron (13). Gili and Gene match Vladimir together (9-10). Gene matches Lee and Uncle Bob together (10-11).

Chromosome 9: Bruce matches DavidD (26.4), with Irene sharing part of that match (13.9). Bruce also matches Dalia (10.7). Bonnie matches Barbara (12.2) and Ron (10.2). Gili matches Jacob (11.8). Gene matches Elaine (11.8).

Chromosome 11: Bruce matches DavidD (12.5). Bruce also matches Elaine (11) on a segment that partially overlaps a match he has with Gili, but Gili and Elaine do not match. Irene matches Herb (16.2) on a segment where she also matches two of my sisters and me (9). Gene matches Julia (15.4) and has nearly congruent matches with Anna and David (~15).

Chromosome 12: Bruce matches Marty (11.9) on a segment partially shared with Gene. Bruce also matches Vladimir (13.2). Gene matches Herb (11.6).

By the way, here is how the Peretz descendants match up with one another.

Total cM/Longest cM					
	Bonnie	Gili	Gene	Irene	Bruce
Bonnie	X	114.2/19.2	118.7/18.6	76.3/12.5	101.0/10.2
Gili	third cousin	X	155.8/25.7	121.5/20.0	83.6/12.9
Gene	third cousin	third cousin	X	127.3/21.4	87.1/8.7
Irene	third cousin	third cousin	third cousin	X	391.2/52.4
Bruce	3C1R	3C1R	3C1R	1C1R	X

Known relationship (vertical label on left)

Figure 20-3

Bonnie's match with Irene is strangely weak, while her match with Bruce is strangely strong.

Chromosome 13: Irene matches Elaine (16.8). Bonnie matches Lloyd (11.8). Gili matches Leonora (10.8).

Chromosome 14: Bonnie matches Elaine (10.9). Gili matches Lloyd (11). Gene matches Rhoda (15.9). Gene also matches Uncle Bob and two of my sisters on two sets of nearly congruent segments—one of just over 12 cM and the other about 5.3 cM.

Chromosome 15: Bruce matches Ron (13.3). Bonnie matches Joe (12.5).

Chromosome 16: Bruce matches Craig (11.5).

Chromosome 17: Gili matches Rita (10) and Rhoda (13.6).

Chromosome 18: Irene matches DavidD (19.1) and Lee (10.9). Bonnie matches Craig (11.9), Rita (12.2), and seven of my close family on nearly congruent segments (~8.2). Gili matches Terry (16.2) and Herb on the same segment (8.4). Gene matches three of my sisters together (~10).

And did you notice that so far we have had no one match three of the Peretz descendants together and only a few that match two of them together?!

Chromosome 20: Bruce matches Aunt Betty (11.4) and Gili shares part of that match. Gili also matches DavidD (11.9). Bonnie matches JudyT (11.6). Gene matches Ralph (14.6).

Chromosome 21: Irene matches Aunt Betty (10.4). Gili and Gene have a small match with Vladimir (6-8).

Chromosome 22: Irene has a match with Sarajoy (12) and me (11). Gili shares those matches (14 each). Bruce and Bonnie appear to as well, but in fact do not. Bonnie matches six others in my family and Rita, all in the same place (7-13), but triangulation is only partial. Bonnie also matches Vladimir (11.8). Gene matches DavidD, JudyT, and Julia (9-11.5) on a single segment, with successful triangulation between JudyT and Julia.

Conclusion

The observation I made after Chromosome 7 above seems largely correct, despite a handful of matches with Jacob and Rita. Peretz' family seems closely connected to the descendants of Mordecai, Isak Fischel, and Isak Josef. It is hard to be more specific than that. My guess is that Berl, who I believe to be Peretz' father, is the younger brother of Isak Josef. That is of course speculation, worthy of no more than a dotted line.

Additional speculation is that Isak Fischel is Peretz' brother.

What is less speculative is that Peretz' family is not closely related to Old Nachman. Nachman is, therefore, probably not a brother of Isak Josef, rather more like a cousin. If I were looking for a reason to upgrade our Y-DNA tests from Y-67 (Filip's and mine) and Y-37 (Zachy's) to Y-111, I have it now. It can wait until the next big sale.

Chromosome 23 – the X chromosome matches

Gene matches three of my sisters on his X chromosome, from 119,402,619 to 127,641,321—11.25 cM. He also matches Uncle Bob on a segment that begins at 119,644,059 and ends in the same place as my sisters—10.66 cM. My sisters and Uncle Bob triangulate successfully, so we know they all get their DNA from the same source. This cannot be a Pikholz or a Kwoczka match as that would require going through my grandfather, and we know that the X is never transmitted from father to son. This segment must have come from my grandmother, which she could have received from any of three of her grandparents. This is endogamy. Gene, a Pikholz descendant, is related to my grandmother.

Gili has matches with Barbara (15.7) and Roslyn (10.2) on the same segment and Aunt Betty (14.2) and Herb (13.8) on another. Both pairs of matches triangulate successfully. Gili also matches Rita (14.3), Rhoda (12), Terry (10.5), and Dalia (16.8). The match with Aunt Betty and Herb is on their Kwoczka side.

163

Bonnie has matches with all four of my sisters (9.5-10.8), a match with JudyT (10.2), and a large collection of smaller matches, many of which are on matching segments.

Chapter Twenty-One

Ron and Craig, and Maybe Someone Else

Over the years, some families have been willing to speak, and some have spoken only when I have spoken to them directly and not always then. Among the silent ones are the children of the brothers Menahem Birnboim and Shlomo Pickholz, the sons of Israel Pickholz and Necha Birnboim of Grzymalow, a town only seven miles (eleven km) from Skalat. Israel and Necha were both born about 1869 according to documents of the International Tracing Service that I found in Yad Vashem.

Menahem Birnboim was born in 1906 and Shlomo Pickholz in 1911. Both died in 1982, and both families live in Israel. I had a brief conversation with Shlomo's son when I first began working on the Pikholz Project. He was not interested even in receiving information from me, but he did refer me to his sister. From her I learned about Menahem, and I subsequently had one brief conversation with his daughter. She said that her father had other brothers and sisters but never agreed to give me additional information.

Some Grzymalow records are in the Skalat record books but most are not, and there are no Grzymalow records to be found on their own. Josef, the son of Uncle Selig, also lived in Grzymalow, which is why we are missing records from that family as well.

A few years into the Pikholz Project, I found Ellis Island records for three young Pikholz women, Cype, Libe, and Leike—known in the United States as Celia, Lena and Laura. In due course, I made contact with a son of Laura and grandchildren of Laura and Lena, and they shared information with me as best they could. Among their recollections was that there were Israeli relatives, whom they were able to identify as Menahem and Shlomo. They also knew that the three sisters had a brother Israel who had been "killed by Cossacks." Between the passenger lists and the New York marriage records, I learned that the parents were Jachiel Pikholz and Gittel Hirschhorn.

When we began looking at DNA, my first thought regarding this family was that Shlomo's son was a candidate for a Y-DNA test. Menahem's only son died during his army service in 1962 at age eighteen. It was only then that I learned that Shlomo's son had died nine years earlier, also in connection with his military service.

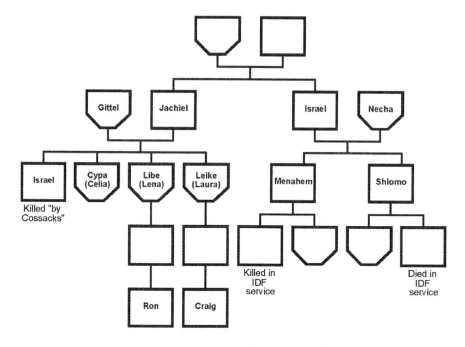

Figure 21-1

When FTDNA had its big sale in December 2014, I decided to make a concerted attempt to get a test from one the last of the children of the three sisters in the U.S.—Laura's son Ed with whom I had had on-and-off correspondence for several years. Ed's son Craig told me that his father had died only a few weeks earlier, but he agreed to do the Family Finder test in his father's stead. Soon after, Lena's grandson Ron tested as well.

The two Israeli cousins are in the generation of Ron and Craig's parents, so they would give us even better results. To date I have not succeeded in getting any response at all from them. We can take this family back only as far as the 1860s and have no idea which Pikholz of the earlier generation might be their particular ancestor.

After receiving the Family Finder results for Craig and Ron, I put them into GEDmatch and compared them to the other Pikholz descendants, excluding those from Rozdol. I was interested in seeing who matched the two cousins together and who matched one cousin in segments of 10 cM or more.

The results, in Figure 21-2, show only two matches with both Craig and Ron and individual matches of 10-21 cM spread across the Pikholz families. But that does not mean that we have nothing to learn from their results.

Craig has overlapping matches with descendants of Nachman Pikholz (1795) on chromosomes 1 and 7. One of the two matches that Craig and Ron share is with David Dekel, from that same family. And both Ron and Craig have individual matches with David, Rita, Rita's cousin Roslyn, and Filip. As I write this analysis, the results from Susan and Maciej's tests are not yet in.

Chr.	Matches with Craig	Matches with Ron	Matches with both
1	Jacob, Filip & DavidD (5-6.2)	DavidD (~20), Rita (15.5), Barbara (11.8)	
2	Rhoda (11.5), Filip (11)	Nan (21)	
4	Leonora (11.5) & Charles (10.7)	Jacob (11 & 10), my family (10)	
5		Lee (15.9), Elaine (13.3)	
7	Filip (13.7) & Roslyn (11), Lloyd (12)	Bruce (10.8) & Gili (6.1)	
8		JudyT (12.5 & 11.2) DavidD (15.7), Gili (13)	
9	Rita (11.7), Marty (10,) Dalia (10.7)	Bonnie (10.2), Leonora 14.1)	
10	Julia (13.6)		
11	DavidD (11.1), Ralph (17.2)	Dalia (10.2)	
12	Anna & David (~13)	JudyT (12.2), Roslyn (12.3)	
13	Julia (10.2)		
14			DavidD (7.7)
15	Joyce (11.3)	Bruce (13.3)	
16	Bruce (11.5), Joyce (11)		
17	Joyce (12.3)	Aunt Betty & my sisters (~10)	
18	Bonnie (11.9), Elaine (11.7)	my family (10-11)	
20			Anna (13.3-13.7)
22	Nan (13.9)		

Figure 21-2

It appears, therefore, that the family of the brothers Jachiel and Israel from Grzymalow may be descendants of Old Nachman. Of course, we cannot draw conclusions without better evidence—and Craig and Ron both match people in other Pikholz lines. Perhaps the Israeli cousins will eventually test and will make the picture clearer.

There is an interesting angle in chromosome 23, the X. Both Craig and Ron are Pikholz through their fathers. Men do not inherit any X from their fathers, so their X is from their mothers. Yet Ron has a match on his X with Charles from

167

Chapter Six, and Craig has X matches with six different Pikholz descendants from all different parts of the family.

These people are related to Craig and Ron via their mothers. Craig's and Ron's mothers. This is endogamy. This same endogamy may account for some of the other matches in Figure 21-2. It's part of the cost of doing business in the world of Jewish genealogy. One family, one people.

There is also something else in these results. Joyce from Kansas City. The family that in Chapter Two appears to be connected to no one else.

Matches between Craig and Joyce				

Minimum threshold size to be included in total - 700 SNPs

Mismatch-bunching Limit - 350 SNPs

Minimum segment cM to be included in total - 1.0 cM

Chr	Start Location	End Location	cM	SNPs
1	27661810	31033624	4.3	917
1	144147102	149615793	3.1	730
1	162785204	165104905	2.6	800
6	31251673	32912195	1.4	2137
6	143954474	148093173	3.7	1139
10	62091197	66566055	3.0	887
12	8887233	19933726	4.2	862
15	31568615	36963367	11.3	1574
16	6778399	11408933	11.0	1903
17	63017961	69049865	12.2	1719

Largest segment = 12.2 cM
Total of segments > 1 cM = 56.7 cM

Matches between Ron and Joyce				

Minimum threshold size to be included in total - 700 SNPs

Mismatch-bunching Limit - 350 SNPs

Minimum segment cM to be included in total - 1.0 cM

Chr	Start Location	End Location	cM	SNPs
1	9350456	13654784	8.6	917
1	28613008	33167118	6.4	1207
1	97711272	101484371	3.5	1068
2	119610102	128285718	9.5	1845
6	47808137	53698034	4.1	1295
8	17602799	19591821	4.2	1059
11	62538497	66442852	3.3	906
12	8887233	11734171	3.6	769

Largest segment = 9.5 cM
Total of segments > 1 cM = 43.1 cM

Figure 21-3

Craig matches Joyce on chromosomes 15, 16, and 17 on segments of 11-12.3 cM. These are segments not to be sneezed at, especially when we have three of them. I did one-to-one comparisons on GEDmatch for Craig and Joyce and Ron and Joyce.

Craig shares 56 cM of DNA with Joyce, and Ron shares 43 cM. Before the FTDNA endogamy adjustments that is considered about third cousin level.

FTDNA's algorithm adjusts Craig and Joyce to fourth-remote cousins and Ron and Joyce to fifth-remote cousins.

Ron and Joyce have three matches of over six cM on chromosomes 1 and 2; segments smaller than Craig's but not insignificant. In addition, both Craig and Ron have a segment that matches Joyce on chromosome 12 that begins at 8,887,233. The segments are small, but the fact that she matches both cousins tells me that this is a real match.

Perhaps Jachiel and Israel are brothers of Joyce's great-grandmother Necha (Nellie) Rochester. Perhaps they are first cousins or further. This is certainly not yet a "solid line" connection, rather one that requires a broken or dotted line. But I think that the most recent common ancestor of these two families will be found after 1820 rather than before.

I would like to see some additional test results, both from Joyce's cousins and Craig and Ron's. But especially from the two cousins in Israel.

Is there more?

Several previous chapters have concluded with the lament that not enough people have tested and the hope, the plea, that perhaps other family members will do Family Finder tests. In this particular case, we may have another option to determine whether Craig and Ron—and perhaps Joyce—are part of the family of Old Nachman Pikholz.

Based on documented relationships and the conclusions of Chapters One, Five and Eight; we have six test kits from descendants of Nachman Pikholz, two of whom are descendants of his son Arie Leib. A third is waiting for test results. Those three—Jacob, Filip and Maciej—could serve as Group 1 for reconstructing the genome of Arie Leib. Jacob and Filip are descendants of his son Josef, and Maciej is a descendant of Arie Leib's daughter Ester Feige. Rita, her cousin Roslyn, Susan, and David Dekel would be Group 2. This Lazarus kit would then be compared to the kits of Craig, Ron, and Joyce to see how likely it is that they are closely related to Arie Leib's family.

Maciej's results were delayed, and I prepared a Lazarus kit without him to see how close it would be to the 1500 cM necessary for batch processing. The Lazarus kit for Arie Leib was not even 300 cM, so it was clear that Maciej's kit would not help much. For this kind of comparison, we would not have needed a batch-processed kit. One-to-one comparisons would have sufficed.

But clearly, 4-500 cM would not be useful for comparing Arie Leib to Craig, Ron, and Joyce.

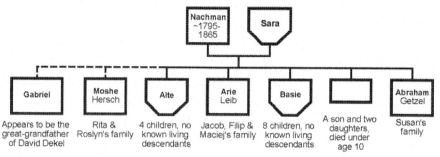

Figure 21-4

Perhaps there are enough other family members who can test. I am not sure. But if there are, they would be useful. When I suggested to Jacob early on that we test Maciej, his reaction was like many novices to genetic genealogy, "But we know he is my third cousin." That, of course, misses the point. In Chapter Seven, we knew that Anna and David are half-siblings and that my sisters and I are full siblings, but the test matches my sisters have with Anna are far better than mine with David. Here too, it's the diversity of cousins that can make the difference. Please cousins, I want some more.

Chapter Twenty-Two

Extreme Ancestors

Footprints, not fingerprints

At the extreme right and left ends of the ancestral tree, we find the all-maternal and all-paternal lines. Those lines are no different from the other ancestral lines in their transmission of the autosomal DNA in the twenty-two pairs of chromosomes, yet each of those lines has sex-specific aspects that affect our ability to use them for research.

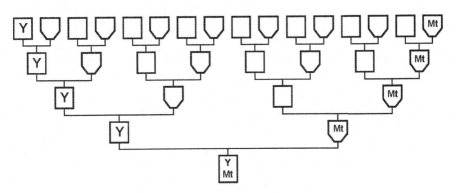

Figure 22-1

Those two lines represent a very small amount of genetic material. If you look at the generation of your great-great-grandparents, they are two of sixteen lines and only a very small part of those two. Go up a generation and they are two of thirty-two. But they are the only lines that are traceable; they leave footprints, not just fingerprints. You know precisely to which ancestors they lead, and they go back in time as far as you could wish.

The Y and mitochondrial DNA from all the ancestors between the two extremes never reach the person at the bottom. So why do I care what Y-DNA came from my mother's side or my other ancestral sides? Those ancestors give me their autosomal DNA, but nothing else. The reason, of course, is that those bits of genetic material can help find relatives on those lines. I want the families of all those in the middle no less than the two extremes. And although my father's mother's maternal line are not my extreme ancestors, they are my father's extreme ancestors.

Most of this book has been about autosomal DNA. But since my family members have done Y-37 or better for five of my eight great-great-grandfathers and full MtDNA for five of my eight great-great-grandmothers, I do not want to conclude without summarizing them and perhaps addressing the possible strategies for research.

Figure 22-2 shows each line, with the ancestral surname, the name of the person who tested and the haplogroup.

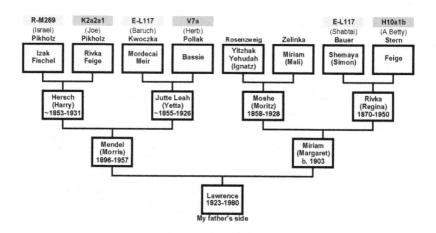

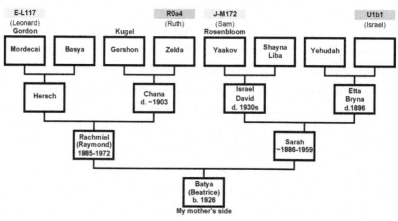

Figure 22-2

The great-great-grandfathers

PIKHOLZ: I have discussed my all-paternal line beginning with Chapter One. I have two perfect matches, one leading to Nachman Pikholz, and one to Mordecai Pikholz. This is as expected. No other match is as close as one mutation away, so although some of the matches from the pre-surname period may be highly relevant, none of those with Y tests is on my all-paternal line.

KWOCZKA: The tester here is my father's second cousin Baruch, whose grandfather is the brother of my great-grandmother. His Y-37 test produced, thus far, eleven matches one mutation away and more than two dozen that are two mutations away. However, only one of all those is as close as a suggested third-fifth cousin according to Family Finder. Therefore, any actual connection to all those matches is quite distant and beyond the limits of our paper trail. For our purposes, the Kwoczka family begins in Zalosce in the mid-1790s, and for the time being it will stay that way.

ROSENZWEIG: We have no candidates for testing in my great-grandfather's Rosenzweig line. My grandmother had three brothers, but two had no children and the third has only granddaughters. My great-grandfather had three brothers, but we know of no male-line descendants among the survivors.

BAUER: My father's second cousin Shabtai tested and has four matches one mutation away and twenty-two matches two mutations away. We know that the Bauer name goes back at least until the early 1800s, and there are quite a few Bauers in Kunszentmiklos (Hungary) where my great-grandmother was born and in Apostag where the Bauers had lived previously.

None of Shabtai's matches has the surname Bauer. This would be almost unthinkable in western, non-Jewish populations where surnames went back much earlier in time and were more stable.

GORDON: My first cousin Leonard did this test. He has five matches, two from a single family, with zero mutations and ten more one mutation away. Here too, none of them is Gordon. Our Gordons go back into the early 1700s according to two distantly-related researchers. One of the zero matches is with a Kapelowitsch family, and we suspect a connection between a family of that name and our Rosenblooms who lived not far from the Gordons. That suspicion appears to be supported by autosomal DNA.

The haplogroup for Leonard, Baruch, and Shabtai is E-L117 despite the fact that the Gordons are from today's Belarus, the Kwoczkas are from east Galicia, and the Bauers are from Hungary. If we look at the thirty-seven markers, the three families share twenty-one of them.

The two that are closest genetically are the Bauers and the Gordons.

Differences: Bauer-Kwoczka 7, Bauer-Gordon 3, Gordon-Kwoczka 8

Figure 22-3

KUGEL: We know nothing about possible descendants of my great-grandmother's known brothers, so we have no one to test.

ROSENBLOOM: As I discussed in Chapter Nine, my second cousin Sam tested and has only three matches total. None is of interest.

Also discussed in Chapter Nine, is that we know nothing about my great-grandmother's family except her father was a Levi.

The great-great-grandmothers

With the great-great-grandmothers, the surname is even less relevant since women's surnames are generally not passed down to their descendants. On the other hand, we expect more matches with MtDNA than with Y-DNA because mitochondrial mutations are fewer and farther between.

PIKHOLZ: My third cousin Joe tested for his maternal line and has eighty-one perfect matches. Twenty-four of these have Family Finder results. Of these, five are suggested third-fifth cousins and one is a suggested second-fourth cousin. Joe's test was done recently and thus far, I have had only preliminary and tentative responses from two of them.

It would be interesting to do an MtDNA test on a Riss (or Baar) descendant to help test the theory that their ancestor Ryfka Pikholz is the same as my Rivka Feige as I suggested in Chapter Twelve. Such a test cannot prove they are the same person, but it can prove that they are not. There is, in fact, one Riss female-line descendant, but she has never responded to me over several years, even without mention of DNA. Neither have her sons thus far.

POLLAK: This is the maternal side of my Kwoczka great-grandmother, and the tester is my father's first cousin Herb. Herb has no perfect matches, but he has about thirty matches that are one mutation away and are all perfect with one another. That one mutation is in an area called the Coding Regions. The mutation, itself, is known as C6925Y. This showed me that our line had mutated away from theirs, perhaps within the last couple of hundred years. That made them worth following up.

Name Haplogroup	HVR1 Mutations	HVR2 Mutations	Coding Region Mutations
Herb V7a	A16129G, G16153A, T16187C, C16189T, T16223C, G16230A,	T72C,G73A T89C,A93G, C146T, C152T,	A769G, A825t, G930A, A1018G, A2758G, C2885T, T3594C, G4104A, T4312C, G4580A, C6925Y, G7146A, T7256C, G7444A, A7521G, T8468C
Herb's group of matches V7a	A16129G, G16153A, T16187C, C16189T, T16223C, G16230A,	T72C,G73A T89C,A93G, C146T, C152T,	A769G, A825t, G930A, A1018G, A2758G, C2885T, T3594C, G4104A, T4312C, G4580A, G7146A, T7256C, G7444A, A7521G, T8468C, T8655C,

Figure 22-4 [figures are intentionally blurred]

Eight of Herb's matches are considered Family Finder matches as well—four of them suggested third-fifth cousins. Nine had not done Family Finder tests at all, and when I approached FTDNA about offering this group of nine a special price, they agreed. Unfortunately, only one of the nine actually took advantage of the offer. You cannot do this kind of research in a vacuum. Your matches have to cooperate.

If we wanted to see if Herb's mutation comes specifically from his mother, we could test one of the first cousins of Rhoda or Terry. Their mothers are Pikholz descendants, unlike Rhoda and Terry whose fathers are the Pikholz descendants. If those cousins have the C6925Y that Herb has, then the mutation came from further up the line.

ZELINKA: We have no known test candidates for this line.

STERN: Aunt Betty did this test and found only nine matches total; only three with zero mutations. All three did Family Finders and none matched. There is nothing remotely familiar in the geography of their ancestors.

GORDON: We do not know anything about the mother of my Gordon great-grandfather. He had no sisters that we know of.

KUGEL: My second cousin Ruth did this test and has fourteen perfect matches. One of these, my research colleague Adam Brown, has Kugel ancestors from the same place. But this test looks at Mrs. Kugel, not the Kugel surname. Adam and Ruth are suggested fourth-remote cousins, so there may be something there.

Of Ruth's remaining thirteen perfect matches, one is a suggested fifth-remote cousin and the rest are off the Family Finder charts.

ROSENBLOOM: We don't know anything about Israel David Rosenbloom's family except his parents' given names. We have no test candidates.

The test results of my maternal line are discussed in detail in Chapter Nine. As I wrote there, this is a long game. We may think we have tested to find matches, but more realistically, we test so that people who test (perhaps many) years later will find us waiting for them. This is particularly true of the ancestral lines at the extremities of our charts.

Chapter Twenty-Three

Chromosome Twenty-Three

The X chromosome

After having been introduced back in Chapter Zero, Chromosome 23 known as "X" has not made many appearances in the subsequent chapters. I would like, therefore, to use this eponymous chapter as an example of how one might work with the X chromosome. I shall use my great-great-grandparents Bassie Pollak and Mordecai Meir Kwoczka to do so.

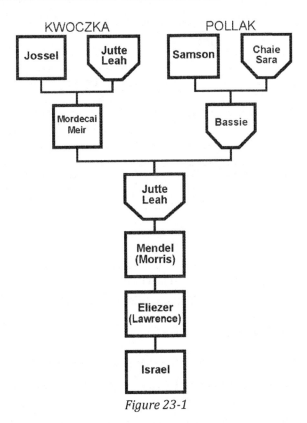

Figure 23-1

Figure 23-1 shows my personal ancestors up through my Kwoczka and Pollak great-great-grandparents, and on to their parents.

As I explained in Chapter Zero, the X chromosome behaves differently in males than in females. Males inherit their single X chromosome intact from their mothers. The parallel inheritance from the father is the Y chromosome. Women have two X chromosomes—one inherited intact from the father and one from the mother after standard recombination. Therefore, a woman carries one X chromosome that is entirely from her paternal grandmother.

There is actually some debate about the recombination of the X, and there is anecdotal evidence that the X is more likely than other chromosomes to be overwhelmingly from one of a woman's maternal grandparents rather than tending to be fifty-fifty. Roberta Estes discusses this at some length.

As a result the number of contributing ancestors does not double with each generation, as with autosomal DNA, but increases in a Fibonacci series— 1, 1, 2, 3, 5, 8, 13 ...) Therefore in any given generation, different ancestors appear in different proportions.

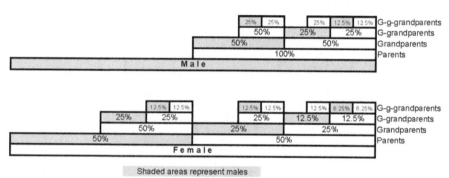

Shaded areas represent males

Figure 23-2

Blaine Bettinger has designed a circular representation of the same phenomenon, which some people find easier to visualize.[1]

Who has Kwoczka-Pollak X-DNA?

Among the descendants of my great-grandmother Jute Leah Kwoczka who have tested, five carry her X-DNA. Those would be Aunt Betty and Herb from my father's generation and Rhoda, Terry, and Lee from my generation. A sixth family member, my third cousin Pinchas, carries Kwoczka-Pollak X-DNA by virtue of descending from one of Jute Leah's brothers. Other descendants are disqualified from this particular analysis because they have two consecutive male ancestors, therefore, they would not carry X from the Kwoczka-Pollak family.

Aunt Betty's son Ed has all his X from his mother, so including him in this analysis would be redundant.

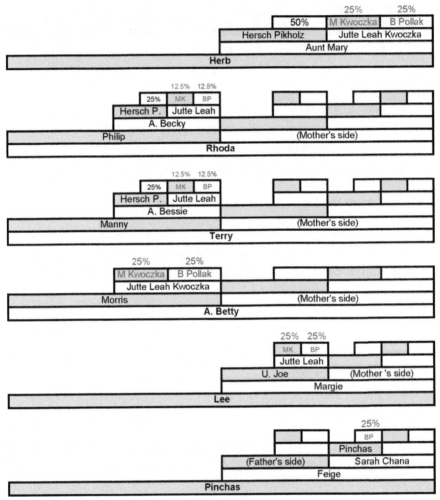

Figure 23-3

As Figure 23-3 shows, Bassie Pollak (BP) and Mordecai Meir Kwoczka (MK) each contribute 25 percent of the X-DNA of Aunt Betty, Herb, and Lee, but only half that much (12.5 percent) of the X-DNA of Rhoda and Terry. Pinchas has the 25 percent from Bassie but nothing from Mordecai Meir.

179

Oddly enough, Pinchas has only one X-match within this group, a triangulated match of 16-17 cM with Aunt Betty and Herb. Since Pinchas has X-DNA from the Pollak side but not the Kwoczka side, this one segment is definitely Pollak. Whether others might be, we cannot tell.

Pinchas' matches with Herb, Lee, Rhoda, Terry, A. Betty

Figure 23-4

We have a few other family members who could participate in this analysis—the first cousins of Rhoda and Terry who I mentioned in the previous chapter. But their lines are all female, so only 6.25 percent comes from each of the great-great-grandparents.

Endogamy from the Zwiebels and the Lewinters

There is one other point I would like to make in order to emphasize the endogamy factor. As I mentioned in Chapter Sixteen, Rhoda and Pinchas have a relationship through their mutual Zwiebel line that has nothing to do with the rest of us.

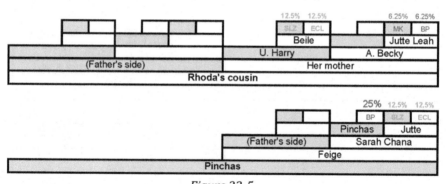

Figure 23-5

Because Rhoda's one first cousin, a female, carries X-DNA from her grandfather Uncle Harry, she and Pinchas received 25 percent of their X-DNA from Shimshon Leib Zwiebel and Ester Chava Lewinter (see the numbers in green.) This is a significant amount, and it could give false positives when comparing their X-DNA with possible matches. Therefore, Rhoda's cousin *must* not be included here.

It is imperative to take this kind of thing into account when designing your analyses.

Analysis

The next step should be to find which other people outside our project match on the same segments of the X that we have determined to be Kwoczka or Pollak segments. GEDmatch has a Tier 1 tool called Matching Segments that does just that. However, it works for only the first twenty-two chromosomes. John at GEDmatch advises:

> *"The algorithm for X matching is somewhat different than the one for autosomal. We don't have any immediate plans to add Chr 23 to the matching segment function."*

Therefore, the only way to do this on GEDmatch is with one-to-one matches, a slow and tedious process.

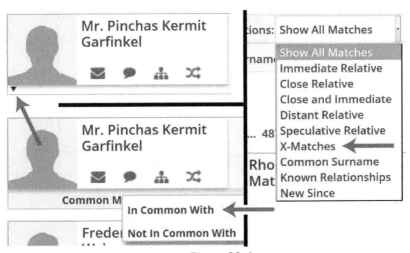

Figure 23-6

I would like to narrow down the matches of interest. Looking at Aunt Betty's match list (4,707 people), there is a way to list only those she has in common with Pinchas, though their matches are not necessarily in the same place. The "in common with" function is on the left side of Figure 23-6. Aunt Betty and Pinchas have 2,462 matches in common.

Another way to go would be looking at all of Aunt Betty's X matches using the "Relations" filter at the top left of her match page. There are 1873 people who match Aunt Betty on the X chromosome. Unfortunately, there is no way to combine the "in common with" with the X-filter.

Of Aunt Betty's 1,873 matches on the twenty-third chromosome, 281 are "suggested third-fifth cousins" or closer. I looked at all 281, and seventeen of them are greater than 5 cM and fall within the location that should match Pinchas. The only one of the seventeen that does is a 5.5 cM segment of someone named Esther. This means that Esther shares Pollak DNA with Aunt Betty, Pinchas, and Herb. It cannot be Kwoczka DNA, because Pinchas has no X-DNA from the Kwoczka side.

Aunt Betty's X-chromosome matches on the segment she shares with Pinchas

Match	Start Location	End Location	cMs	Matches Pinchas	Matches Herb	Matches JudyT
Herb	18,581,210	43,698,823	40.3	16.0	-	
Pinchas	30,046,242	39,546,250	16.8	-	16.0	
Edith	32,072,616	37,918,950	10.5		10.1	
Deborah R.	32,766,712	39,971,372	9.3		5.9	
Ruth R.	30,394,927	32,843,429	8.7			
Mindy	32,473,409	37,474,122	7.4			
Roni	31,180,365	32,760,981	7.0		7.0	
Doris	33,499,489	39,658,806	6.3			
Esther	32,847,302	37,918,950	5.9	5.5	5.5	
Jarmila	29,623,359	32,201,655	5.8			
Marcia	33,301,665	39,137,763	5.6			
JudyT	32,847,302	37,606,995	5.5			-
Sabrina	33,039,414	38,094,186	5.5			5.1
Yudita	33,039,414	38,094,186	5.5			
Rufina	29,623,359	32,135,494	5.4			
Lee	32,847,302	37,474,122	5.3			
Marlene	33,039,414	37,918,950	5.2			
J.S.	29,801,794	32,135,494	5.1			
Steven	29,801,794	32,135,494	5.1			

JudyT is a Pikholz descendant, but not known to be a Kwoczka or Pollak.

Figure 23-7

The other sixteen people—those who match Aunt Betty but not Pinchas—must be on Aunt Betty's mother's side. But that cannot be either, as three of Aunt Betty's matches—Edith, Deborah, and Roni—also match Herb.

There is obviously something else going on here. Perhaps it's the way we understand the X chromosome or the way FTDNA does the analysis or my own understanding (or lack of understanding). Whichever is the case, I think it is useful to shine a light on what appears to be a problem. I would like to think that new tools will be developed to make this analysis easier.

Figure 23-8 shows the rest of the matches within the family on the X chromosome. The green lines where Herb and Lee match must be Kwoczka-Pollak DNA, because Lee has no X-DNA from the Pikholz side.

The other areas are highly likely to be Kwoczka-Pollak DNA, though each combination lends itself to certain other possibilities. If (when?) we have a matching-segment tool, there will be any number of things to do here regarding matches with matches who are not know to be relatives.

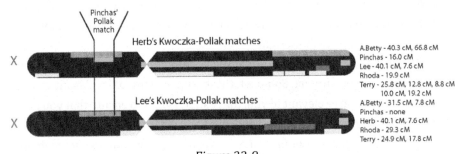

Figure 23-8

---

1 http://www.thegeneticgenealogist.com/2008/12/21/unlocking-the-genealogical-secrets-of-the-x-chromosome/

A Stopping Place

Are we done yet?

How do I know when I am finished? Research is ongoing, so there is never really a point where I can say that the time to publish has come, that I have reached a conclusion.

I still have unachieved goals and unfulfilled plans—there are even family members whose tests results are pending and could be used here with a few more weeks of patience. I have, however, reached what my mother used to call "a stopping place." Twenty-three chapters for twenty-three pairs of chromosomes sounds about right.

If it is not a conclusion in the sense of completion, there are nonetheless conclusions to be drawn. Some of those conclusions are relevant to my research. Others are relevant to you, the reader. I want to ensure that you have the opportunity to absorb the lessons that I have learned.

The question asked of me most frequently is "How did you get so many family members to test?" The answer to that question goes back five, ten, fifteen years ago or more. A while back, I received an inquiry from someone who matched one of the Rozdol Pikholz descendants on GEDmatch. The match was only with him, so I was sure it was from one of his "other sides."

I wrote and asked him about the families of his mother and grandmother. He wasn't interested. In fact, he explained, he wasn't interested in his Pikholz side either. He only tested because he respected the work I have been doing, sending out summaries a couple of times a year for fifteen-plus years, gathering information about his family that might someday interest his grandchildren, visiting the New York and New Jersey graves of his parents and grandparents, and putting them on the Pikholz Project website. And this was not even someone I had asked to test, but rather someone who responded to a general request for participants.

So how do you get so many people to test? First get into your time machine and start years ago, building the relationships, the respect for your work. The only participant in my projects who came out of the blue is Milton, whose family I had never heard of until November 2014.

Much of my personal genealogy research is what they call Single-Surname Research. That is different from what most people do and in some respects is much harder. In particular, you, the researcher, are not the center of the universe. You have to consider the family structure from multiple vantage points. But you almost have to do some of that in genetic research, and adjusted forms of the lessons learned here can be transferred to "traditional" genealogy research.

The database and the web site

My personal research has two levels of organization—my database and my website. The database resides on my own computer, with appropriate backups, and consists of information that I have determined to my own satisfaction to be fact. If I am not certain that two people are brothers, I do not record them as brothers. If I am not certain that a death record pertains to a particular known individual, I do not record that date for that person.

I cannot say too often that I know that once I record something in my database, I will not revisit it later. Nor will my research heirs, should I be so fortunate as to have any. I am the expert on my own research, and if I write it down anyone using my work will expect it to be correct. To be sure, I make many a note in the comments beginning with "perhaps," "likely" or "almost certainly."

In my website, I am a bit more liberal. There is where I tell a story, whether with text, diagrams, photographs, or documents. I do not really understand how people can opt for merging the database and the website—even without the new custom of turning it over to an online company for safekeeping and manipulation.

As I have acknowledged in other formats, it takes extra work to maintain both the database and the website. The online sites which allow researchers to put everything one place are probably much easier, but it is not my way.

Most of the conclusions I have drawn from the preceding chapters do not yet reach the level of certainty that I need for my database, even though such conclusions are good enough for my website because even without full documentation I know they are correct.

Progress in Skalat

Back in the Introduction (Figure i-2), I had identified eighteen Pikholz families from Skalat. Some of these appeared closely related, while the near-certain relationships with others were not clear. Two of the eighteen families have no living descendants.

Two other families—Milton's great-grandmother Sarah and Gabriel of Husiatyn—were added to the group during the course of our genetic research.

One way to measure success is by the mergers within that group of twenty.

I shall leave aside the Y-DNA results that show a common ancestor for Nachman (1795), Mordecai (1805), and Isak Fischel (~1820), and the analysis of Peretz in Chapter Twenty which has helped inch forward with the understanding of those Y results. The autosomal testing for Skalat has allowed me to make the following determinations. The very high probability determinations are in bold.

- **Sara bat Moshe Hersch is the younger sister of Berisch ben Moshe Hersch**, probably from both parents. (*Chapter Six*)
- That same Moshe Hersch (~1812) is the son of Izak Josef (1784). (*Chapter Six*)
- **Szulim, the husband of Sara bat Moshe Hersch, is the brother of Simon and both are the sons of Mordecai (1805).** (*Chapter Thirteen*)
- **Moshe Hersch (~1825) is the son of Nachman (~1795).** (*Chapter Five*)
- Gabriel (~1822) is the son of Nachman, and Moshe (~1851) is the son of Gabriel. (*Chapter Eight*)
- **Josef (~1860) is actually Itzig Josef, the son of Uncle Selig, who is in turn the son of Izak Josef (1784).** (*Chapter Seven*) We already know that Izak Josef is the father-in-law of Isak Fischel.
- **Sarah (early 1840s) is the sister of Breine, who we know to be the daughter of Ryfka (b. 1815-20?).** (*Chapter Twelve*)

Twenty Skalat families with four or more generations
The names that are underlined were added during the project.
Shaded families have no known living descendants.

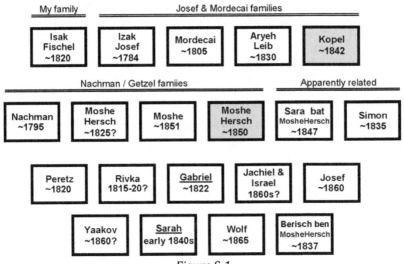

Figure S-1

My conclusions have reduced the number of Skalat families from twenty to twelve. However, two of the twelve have no living descendants and two others have thus far declined to test. So they must remain outside the scope of this study.

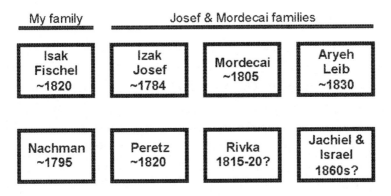

Figure S-2

There are additional determinations that I would have to call speculative. The family of Jachiel and Israel (1860s) may be descendants of Nachman, but it is premature to give credence to this speculation. Ryfka (1815-1820) may be the same person as Rivka Feige, the wife of Isak Fischel and daughter of Izak Josef. A determination here is also premature, though I believe it to be correct. I discussed these two speculative determinations in Chapters Twenty-One and Twelve.

Even more speculative is the possibility (Chapter Thirteen) that Mordecai is the son-in-law of Isak Josef, in addition to being a blood relative.

I mention these speculations only because without DNA tests, I would not even have considered them as possible familial connections. The Family Finder tests opened up new vistas for research and testing.

Lazarus kits

If I hadn't had some experience with Kitty Cooper's mapping tool, assigning segments of DNA to specific ancestors, I might have thought that the Lazarus tool offered by GEDmatch was nothing more than a gimmick. When I saw that I could actually recreate most of my father's genome, I moved along to my grandparents and great-grandparents, eventually building a kit for my great-grandfather that represented 31 percent of his DNA. His two Pikholz parents made it easier, not harder. The creation of the Lazarus kits in Chapters Fifteen and Sixteen involved analysis and decision-making regarding who is related to whom (and how), and what endogamous relationships should be removed from the Lazarus process.

I imagined that such a kit would be helpful in seeing how the other Skalat Pikholz families fit together, and that perhaps it might tell me a thing or two about our relationship with certain non-Pikholz relationships. I tested my great-grandfather's kit in Chapters Seventeen and Eighteen with mixed, though encouraging, results.

What I hadn't envisioned was looking at the matches between the Rozdol Pikholz families and my great-grandfather. The results of that analysis enable me to say with greater confidence that the Pikholz families from Skalat and Rozdol are one family, not just the matching of garden-variety endogamous families.

GEDmatch has provided an important service in Lazarus, and I would like to think that as additional family members test I will be able to use it to test additional hypotheses.

Wish list

The book ends but the research goes on. Going forward, I want to shore up the weaker spots, and I want to look at the parts of the families that have not participated until now. I am hoping that the existence of this book will move some family members to test, but I will still need to convince many of them.

Although often results are unexpected, even serendipitous, the best research comes with planning. Here are some DNA tests that I want for the next round along with my rationales. Unless stated otherwise, these are autosomal tests.

1. Nachum Leib Pikholc was probably born around 1860 and lived in Russia, just north of east Galicia. His few known descendants lived in different places, including in Ukraine east of Kiev. We know of three living great-grandchildren—two brothers and a sister. After two years of discussion, one brother did both a Y-37 test and a Family Finder. However, his concern for privacy got the better of him, and he did not authorize the release of his results. He can't even see them himself.

2. There is only one female-line Riss descendant, and she has three sons with very common names. I would like to make contact with one of the four for an MtDNA test. Such a test might help us learn if their Ryfka and my Rivka Feige is indeed the same person. It could prove they are not. I would like to get some additional Family Finder tests on both sides of the Riss-Baar family. One is on the way.

3. The three living descendants of Gabriel and Sara Pikholz from Husiatyn, as I discussed in Chapters Eight.

4. Two or three of David Dekel's first cousins, in particular the one whose father has no known Jewish DNA.

5. Barbara's cousins (Chapter Thirteen)—both first cousins and second cousins. I also want a Y-37 test from the one male-line descendant of Barbara's great-grandfather Simon Pikholz.

6. At least two more of the Kansas City Pikholz family. I'd like to think that Joyce's relatively weak matches are an anomaly.

7. My father has two living first cousins. One, Herb, has figured prominently in my analyses here. The other has not responded to

my requests to test. I have not lost sleep over this because his half-brother's son Marty has tested, so Uncle Dave is represented in our project. But some of Marty's matches are significantly different— usually stronger—than the other second cousins. Therefore, I would really like to get his uncle's participation. I am not sure what I am looking for, but then I rarely am.

8.   Sarit. Her mother was born in Lwow in 1920 to Markus and Sara Pikholz. We know nothing about either, including which one is the Pikholz. Lwow was "the big city," so the family could have come from either Rozdol or Skalat.

9.   A Y-37 and at least two Family Finders from the one other Skalat-area family with an existing male-line. This family lives in Israel and has not been receptive, though one descendant in the US said she would do a Family Finder.

10. A few more descendants of Nachman (1795), including Rita's cousins. There are not many candidates, but I would like to see a bit more diversity. One person from the older generation has a test kit in hand.

11. Leonora's sister, just because that family has so many Pikholz connections.

12. Some of Lloyd's cousins. This family, descendants of Mordecai and Taube, is older than the others so the living descendants are further from the source. Here too, one older cousin has a test kit in hand.

13. Some of Dalia's cousins.

14. Other descendants of Mordecai and Taube, whose families are not represented here at all. Starting with at least one with a Zellermayer connection.

15. The two Israeli cousins of the fathers of Craig and Ron. And Craig's uncle.

16. Rose Pikholz married Jack Lifschultz. They had three children in Kharkov in the 1890s. The American-Israeli descendant I had been emailing with disappeared some years ago.

17. Anyone we can get from the Rozdol Pikholz families. We have twelve, and I would like to have thirty to forty. I would particularly like to get Y-37 tests from the three Rozdol families who have not tested at all.

18. I would like to upgrade the three Y-37 tests we have from Rozdol to Y-111. And the three Skalat Y tests as well. Next time they have a sale perhaps.

19. More Kwoczka cousins. There are candidates among the descendants of both brothers of my great-grandmother. I'd like to get a few from each group.

20. Two or three Rosenbloom cousins of my generation.

21. A few more of the Gordons of my generation. The project there would eventually be the wider Gordon family.

22. There are so few close candidates among my grandmother's Rosenzweigs, Zelinkas and Bauers—but this is a wish list, so I can wish.

Thoughts at the buzzer

- Test everyone you can.
- Don't concentrate on the small segments, but don't ignore them either.
- "We are all cousins" is nice as a slogan, but in fact, most of us have maybe 4,000 to 5,000 matches meaning we don't match many other people. We don't even match some of our known relatives.

  For some, that slogan is a way to express frustration. For others, it's an excuse to avoid getting down on hands and knees and seeing what can be done.
- You don't know less than what I knew two years ago. You can do this!
- Your families are all one family. Our people are all one family.

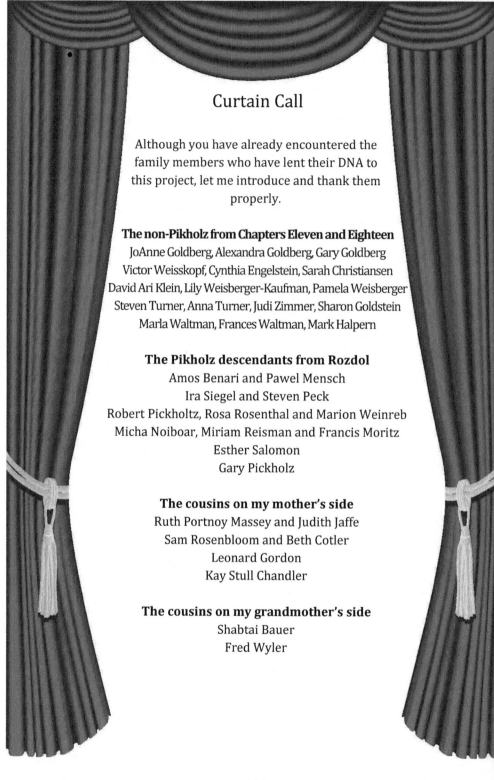

Curtain Call

Although you have already encountered the family members who have lent their DNA to this project, let me introduce and thank them properly.

The non-Pikholz from Chapters Eleven and Eighteen
JoAnne Goldberg, Alexandra Goldberg, Gary Goldberg
Victor Weisskopf, Cynthia Engelstein, Sarah Christiansen
David Ari Klein, Lily Weisberger-Kaufman, Pamela Weisberger
Steven Turner, Anna Turner, Judi Zimmer, Sharon Goldstein
Marla Waltman, Frances Waltman, Mark Halpern

The Pikholz descendants from Rozdol
Amos Benari and Pawel Mensch
Ira Siegel and Steven Peck
Robert Pickholtz, Rosa Rosenthal and Marion Weinreb
Micha Noiboar, Miriam Reisman and Francis Moritz
Esther Salomon
Gary Pickholz

The cousins on my mother's side
Ruth Portnoy Massey and Judith Jaffe
Sam Rosenbloom and Beth Cotler
Leonard Gordon
Kay Stull Chandler

The cousins on my grandmother's side
Shabtai Bauer
Fred Wyler

192

The Kwoczka cousins
Pinchas Garfinkel (Fleischman)
Bruce (Baruch) Francis

The Pikholz descendants
we haven't figured out yet
Joyce Strain
Vladimir Pigoltz

And the Pikholz descendants from Skalat

Descendants of Nachman Pikholz (1795)
Rita Margolies and Roslyn Kuslansky
David Dekel
Susan Chevlowe and Maciej Karczewski
Joanna Lech and Filip Lech
Jacob Laor

Descendants of Jachiel Pikholz
Craig Ball and Ron Weissman

Descendants of Peretz Pikholz
Bonnie Shapot and Gili Mehr
Eugene Trabitz and Bruce Scharf
Irene Scharf

Descendants of Mordecai (1805) and Taube Pikholz
Lloyd Madansky and Judith Tomasik
Barbara Marenus
Dalia Kaplan and Yitzhak Zach Pickholz

Descendants of Moshe Hersch Pikholz
Leonora Sokalsky and Charles Aptowitzer
Nanette Barcus, Carolyn Boles and Steven Barcus
Jane Zeitschel
Stephen Pickholtz

Descendants of Uncle Selig
Anna Lippman
David Lipski

The Riss-Baar cousins
Milton Baar
Julia Riss
Mr. X

My Pikholz third cousins
Elaine Myers and Ralph Goldstein
Joseph Pells

My close Pikholz cousins
Lee Spector, Marty Pickholtz and Ed Goldman
Rhoda Mathias and Terry Kraus

My sisters
Jean Moskowitz
Judith Bohm
Amy Kritzman
Sarajoy Pickholtz

And finally
Cousin Herb Braun
My uncle, Bob Pickholtz
My aunt, Betty Fay Goldman
I thank you all.

Appendix A

People in My Personal Family Mentioned in this Book
PIKHOLZ & KWOCZKA
Those whose names are shaded have done DNA tests

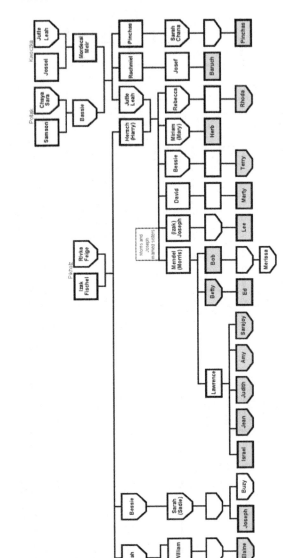

Endogamy:

- The husbands of Leah and Mary (aunt and niece) are uncle and nephew.
- Rebecca's husband's maternal grandmother and Sarah Chana's paternal grandmother are sisters.
- (Izak) Josef Pickholz and his brother Mendel (Morris) married sisters.

195

Appendix B

People in My Personal Family Mentioned in this Book
ROSENZWEIG & ZELINKA, BAUER & STERN
People whose names are shaded have done DNA tests.

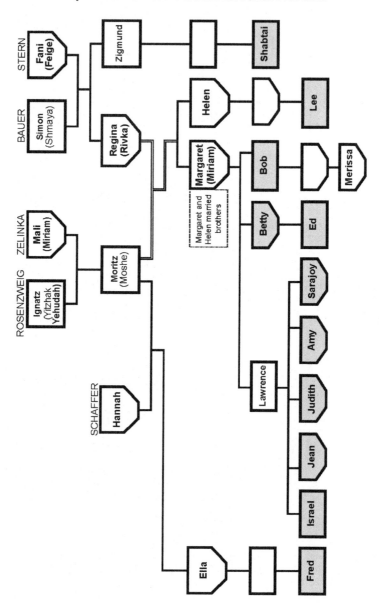

Appendix C

People in My Personal Family Mentioned in this Book
ROSENBLOOM, GORDON & KUGEL
People whose names are shaded have done DNA tests.

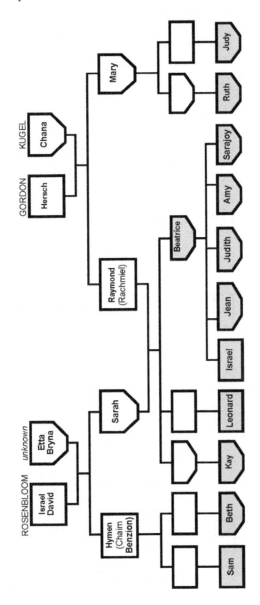

Appendix D

THE ROZDOL PIKHOLZ FAMILIES

People whose names are shaded have done DNA tests.

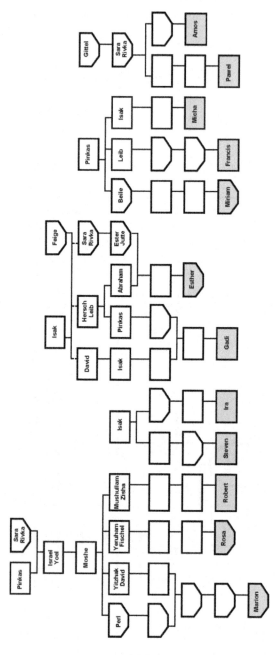

Appendix E

Town Coordinates and Index

The coordinates and distances for the eastern European locations mentioned below are based on the JewishGen Gazetteer, which can be found at http://www.jewishgen.org/Communities/LocTown.asp.

Coordinates are North and East unless otherwise specified.

Page numbers follow each town named, with the exception of Skalat and Rozdol which were too numerous to mention.

Location	Country (today)	Coordinates	Miles (kilometers) from other locations
My ancestors' towns in Galicia			
Skalat	Ukraine	4926 2559	18.7 (30.1) ESE of Tarnopol
Rozdol	Ukraine	4928 2404	26.1 (42) S of Lwow
Podkamen [pages xv, xvii]	Ukraine	4956 2519	10.6 (17) WSW of Zalosce
Zalosce [pages xiv, xv, xvi, 22, 173]	Ukraine	4947 2522	36.7 (59) NW of Skalat
Other towns in Galicia			
Husiatyn [pages 65, 66, 67, 186, 189]	Ukraine	4904 2613	27.4 (44.1) SSE of Skalat
Jagielnica [pages 97, 98]	Ukraine	4857 2544	35.6 (57.3) SSW of Skalat
Grzymalow [pages 165, 167]	Ukraine	4920 2602	7.3 (11.7) SSE of Skalat
Klimkowce [pages xiii, 9, 10]	Ukraine	4936 2606	12.6 (20.3) NNE of Skalat
Kopicienice [page 107]	Ukraine	4906 2556	23.1 (37.2) S of Skalat
Kozowka [page 40, 41]	Ukraine	4926 2509	37.4 (60.2) W of Skalat
Lwow [pages xiii, xix, xx (end note), 29, 66, 190]	Ukraine	4951 2402	26.1 (42) N of Rozdol 85.7 (148.1) WNW of Skalat

Location	Country (today)	Coordinates	Miles (kilometers) from other locations
Podwoloczysk [page 65]	Ukraine	4932 2609	10.2 (16.4) NE of Skalat
Proszowa [page 40]	Ukraine	4927 2532	20.2 (32.6) W of Skalat
Stryj [pages xiv, 29]	Ukraine	4915 2351	17.9 (28.7) SSW of Rozdol
Tarnopol [pages xiv, xx (end note), 56]	Ukraine	4933 2537	18.7 (30.1) WNW of Skalat

East of Galicia

Location	Country	Coordinates	Miles (kilometers)
Nemerow [pages 17, 18, 20]	Ukraine	4858 2850	132.6 (213.4) ESE of Skalat
Czernovitz [pages 66, 107]	Ukraine	4818 2556	78.3 (126.0) S of Skalat
Odessa [pages 17, 18, 46]	Ukraine	4628 3044	300 (483) SE of Skalat
Tetiev [pages 17, 20]	Ukraine	4923 2940	165.5 (266) E of Skalat
Tulcin [pages 13, 16 (end note), 17]	Ukraine	4841 2852	140 (226) ESE of Skalat
Zhvanets [page 111]	Ukraine	4833 2620	65.3 (105.1) SSE of Skalat

Others

Location	Country	Coordinates	Miles (kilometers)
Visk [page 31]	Ukraine	4803 2325	102 (164) SSW of Rozdol 150.7 (242.6) SW of Skalat
Penza [page 73, 74]	Russia	5312 4500	715 (1151) E of Minsk
Borisov [pages 73, 76, 78]	Belarus	5414 2830	44.2 (71.4) ENE of Minsk

Appendix F

Given Names

I am certain that no one reading this book needs an appendix to learn that Esther and Ester, Sarah and Sara, David and Dawid, Josef, Jozef and Joseph and others are simply variations in spelling and not different names. Similarly, most of you do not need me to tell you that the Hebrew Avraham, Aharon, and Shimon are the same as the secular Abraham, Aaron and Simon.

I would, however, like to clarify that certain names appear in this book in different ways, whether due to spelling, language, nicknames, or just the preference of a local scribe. Keep in mind that a person's name may be spelled differently in different documents or even within a single document.

This is not a comprehensive list, but it should cover what you need to get through this book. It is not meant to include names that were adopted in western countries, such as Bernard, Harry, Max, and Morris. Neither does it include names ending with both "a" and "e" such as Chana and Chane.

Men's Names

Ber, Berl, Berisch, Dov

Hersch, Hirsch, Herschel, Zvi

Mordecai, Motie, Mordka, Mordche. This Jewish name is closely affiliated with the secular names Markus and Max.

Isak, Izak, Isaac, Isaak, Eisig, Itzig, Itzik, Yitzhak

Aharon, Aron, Uryn, Aaron

Moshe, Moses

Yaakov, Jakob, Jacob, Kopel

Szulim, Shalom

Women's Names

Dwojre, Dwora, Deborah, Devorah

Rivka, Rifka, Ryfka, Riwke, Rebecca, Becky

Sarah, Sure

Breine, Brana.

Chana, Hannah, Anna

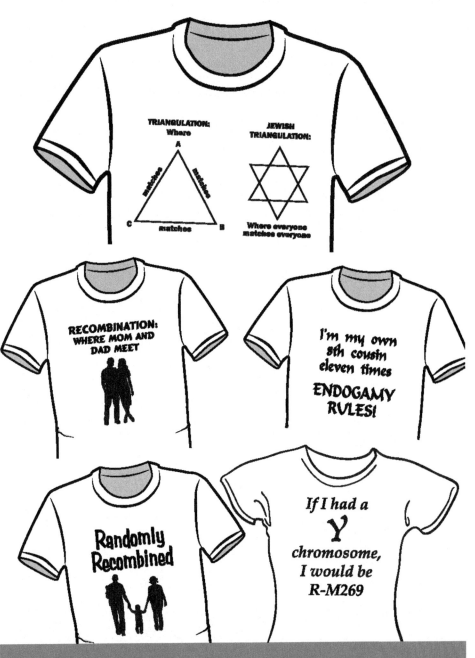

92~
PI(
z **WITHDRAWN**

DATE DUE

AUG 2 3 2016	
SEP 1 8 2016	

PRINTED IN U.S.A.

CPSIA information can be obtained at www.ICGtesting.com
Printed in the USA
BVOW11s2148091215

429180BV00083B/175/P